CARRIERS

MODERN AIR POWER

CARRIERS

Antony Preston

GALLERY BOOKS
An imprint of W.H. Smith Publishers Inc.
112 Madison Avenue
New York, New York 10016

Published by Gallery Books
A Division of W H Smith Publishers Inc.
112 Madison Avenue
New York, New York 10016

Produced by
Brompton Books Corp.
15 Sherwood Place
Greenwich, CT 06830

ISBN 0-8317-6060-5

Printed in Hong Kong

10 9 8 7 6 5 4 3 2 1

TOP RIGHT: A Seacat
short range SAM
leaves its launcher.

TOP RIGHT: A catapult
controller about to
give the signal to
launch an A-6 Intruder.

BOTTOM: The USS
John F Kennedy at
speed.

INSET: The new Soviet
carrier Baku reflected
in the visor of a Royal
Navy helicopter
crewman.

MAIN SPREAD: Sea
Kings and Sea Harriers
on the deck of HMS
Hermes in the South
Atlantic in 1982.

BELOW: The Soviet
Navy's Baku is the
fourth in a series of
four Kiev class hybrid
cruiser/carriers. She
operates Yak-36
'Forger' VTOL aircraft
and ASW helicopters.

RIGHT: The veteran
British carrier Hermes
was sold to India in
1986. Renamed Viraat,
she sailed for Bombay
the following year.

CONTENTS

Almost from the first the apostles of naval air power could foresee the revolution which aircraft would bring about in naval affairs. Nor were they disappointed. Even the primitive aircraft and seaplane carriers which served in World War I achieved remarkable results, and by 1918 the three major naval powers, Great Britain, the United States and Japan, all had designs for true aircraft carriers — ships capable of flying off and recovering wheeled aircraft with the same performance as contemporary land-planes.

Despite peacetime retrenchment naval aviation proceeded apace, but the aviators faced fierce opposition from the proponents of traditional battlefleet tactics. To the 'battleship admirals' the gun-armed battleship was still the core of sea power, and the carrier was there to provide spotting for the guns and reconnaissance to bring the enemy fleet to battle. Even more potent enemies were the advocates of land air power, who claimed that the 'indivisibility of air power' rendered sea power superfluous.

A dedicated band of naval aviators, however, continued to promote the concept of the aircraft carrier as the main striking unit, with the surface fleet providing protection to such 'task forces'. By a strange irony the British, whose empire depended on sea power, had chosen to form a unified Royal Air Force with control over naval aviation in 1918. The resulting inter-service rivalry for scarce resources was never satisfactorily resolved, and left the Navy very weak in aircraft carriers and high-performance aircraft.

The only other navy to operate carriers in the interwar period was the French, but lack of money prevented much from being done. Only one carrier joined the fleet, and plans to build two modern carriers perished with the fall of France in June 1940.

Eventually it was the weakest of the three major naval air arms which was to prove the validity of carrier doctrines. In November 1940 the Royal Navy's Mediterranean Fleet launched a carrier air strike against the Italian Fleet in its main base at Taranto. A small force of Swordfish biplane torpedo-bombers severely damaged several battleships and heavy cruisers with only trifling loss to themselves.

The lesson of Taranto was not lost on the Japanese, who achieved an even more effective blow against the US Pacific Fleet at Pearl Harbor in December 1941. A task force of six carriers took the base by surprise, and a well-co-ordinated torpedo and bombing attack sank two battleships and severely damaged four more. Once again, a powerful surface fleet had been rendered impotent by the striking power of carrier aircraft.

Pearl Harbor did not destroy American sea power. It did, however, compel the Pacific Fleet to make the carrier task forces the spearhead, and henceforward the role of battleships was increasingly confined to escorting the carriers and providing gunfire support for amphibious landings.

In the European theater the demand was for aircraft to support convoys, and in 1941 the first 'escort carriers' appeared, mercantile hulls equipped with flight decks to operate anti-submarine aircraft. The shortage of fleet carriers led to these 'Woolworth carriers' being used to support amphibious landings as well, and by the end of the war they were an integral part of the American and British carrier forces.

The anti-submarine war also saw the first tentative use of helicopters. In 1944 trials

CHAPTER ONE

Early Carriers

took place with an American Sikorsky helicopter flying off the deck of a British merchantman. Although of limited success, these tests foreshadowed the revolution in naval warfare brought about by helicopters a decade later.

After their victory over the Italians at Taranto the venerable Swordfish biplane torpedo bombers earned immortality for their decisive role in stopping the German battleship *Bismarck* in May 1941. After sinking the battlecruiser HMS *Hood* there was nothing to stop the German ship from breaking out into the Atlantic until the carrier *Ark Royal* and her Swordfish arrived on the scene.

But it was the fast carrier task forces which carried the war to Japan, ranging across the vast distances of the Pacific and striking at widely separated targets. In 1942 the first carrier versus carrier battles were fought, the inconclusive Battle of the Coral Sea, followed by the strategically decisive Battle of

LEFT: A Blackburn B5 Baffin flying over HMS *Eagle* in 1935. RAF control over naval aviation caused a near fatal decline, and the return to RN control came too late to re-equip the Fleet Air Arm with high performance aircraft.

Midway. At the Coral Sea the American carriers suffered a 25 percent tactical defeat but managed to frustrate Japanese plans to attack Australia; at Midway three skilfully handled American carriers destroyed the cream of the Japanese navy's carriers and their magnificent aircrews. The carriers lost at Midway could be replaced, and so could the aircraft but the Imperial Japanese Navy could not streamline the training process which had given them the most highly trained aircrews in the world. In the Battle of the Philippine Sea in June 1944, the hapless Japanese pilots were shot down in such numbers that the American pilots dubbed it the 'Great Marianas Turkey Shoot'. A year later the only tactic left to the Japanese was the *kamikaze* dive on to the flight decks of American and British carriers.

As the Japanese naval air arm waned in

LEFT: An Albacore torpedo bomber takes off from the new armored deck carrier HMS *Victorious*.

BELOW: The French training carrier *Jeanne d'Arc* operated three Loire-Nieuport 130 seaplanes.

RIGHT: The rugged US Navy aircraft were well suited to the rigors of carrier landings.

BELOW RIGHT: British armored carriers had many good features but were hampered by the lack of high performance aircraft.

ABOVE: British Seafire fighters were too fragile for carrier flying but provided much needed performance.

LEFT: The US Navy's *Essex* class were the backbone of the fast carrier task forces in 1944-45.

ABOVE RIGHT: Carriers overtook battleships in size cost and complexity by the end of World War II.

RIGHT: Heavily influenced by USN methods and tactics, British carriers played a growing role in the overthrow of Japan in 1945.

effectiveness, the Americans' power increased. A huge pilot training program matched the extraordinary exertions of the aircraft factories and the shipyards, so there was never a lack of aircraft or pilots. By 1944 the performance advantages enjoyed by Japanese pilots had disappeared as well, giving the fast carrier task forces the power to inflict devastation on both the Imperial Japanese Navy and land targets too.

By the late stages of the war the techniques of carrier warfare had advanced beyond anything imagined prewar. Radar provided carriers with a degree of control over air operations, particularly in defense. It became possible to operate all-fighter carriers, and even night fighter carriers, freeing larger ships for strikes against land targets. In 1944-45 the US Navy achieved what had long been regarded as impossible, the defeat of a land-based air force by carrier aircraft alone. More than that, carrier aircraft in all theaters had sunk thousands of enemy ships and submarines. They had also provided vital cover to all the amphibious landings and had saved thousands of lives.

Carrier aviation was not invented in World War II, but it advanced from a crude method of warfare to the most effective contribution to the war at sea. By August 1945 there was no doubt that the big fleet carrier was the capital ship of the future.

Although the aircraft carrier had emerged as the new capital ship at the end of World War II, the nuclear holocaust unleashed on Japan was seen by many defense planners as the precursor of a nuclear age in which only air power would be decisive. The carrier, it was argued, would be wiped out by nuclear bombs before she could launch her aircraft. Thus the US Navy was in the strange position of possessing the most powerful carrier force in the world, yet facing accusations that its carriers had no wartime role. There were 26 of the magnificent *Essex* class in commission or completing, eight light fleet carriers (CVLs) converted from light cruisers as an emergency measure, and 70 escort carriers (CVEs), backed up by over 40,000 aircraft. There were also three new carriers, the 45,000-ton *Midway* class, under construction.

In the face of the nuclear threat there was strong support for a rationalization of the defense establishment. In the eyes of the US Air Force this meant taking over the US Army Air Force, while the Army looked enviously at the US Marine Corps, which had its own air element. Despite the 1947 National Security Act which created three separate services (creating the fully independent USAF) the exponents of extreme air power continued to lobby against the 'costly duplication' of a separate naval air force.

The Air Force argued that mere possession of nuclear weapons, bombs dropped by intercontinental long-range bombers, would deter aggression and thereby eliminate the need for powerful naval and land forces. It was seductively simple, but merely echoed the flawed thinking of air power enthusiasts such as Mitchell and Trenchard between the wars. Inter-service rivalry reached a new pitch when, in April 1949, the USAF succeeded in persuading the Secretary of Defense to cancel a new giant carrier, only five days after her keel had been laid.

The new ship, to be named the *United States,* was a direct challenge to the Air Force. She would have been large enough to operate twin-engined bombers capable of attacking Soviet land targets with nuclear weapons, and the Air Force saw this as a deliberate duplication of their own strategic bombing effort. The Secretary for the Navy, John L Sullivan, resigned in protest at what he saw as an assassination attempt against the Navy. Air Force lobbyists did nothing to suppress rumors of a reduction of the US Navy's air element or even its transfer to the USAF, and the abolition of the US Marine Corps.

The Navy's case was that its carrier air power provided much more flexibility. The pattern of future wars could not be predicted, and the United States dared not assume that the next conflict would be an all-out nuclear war. Carriers would enable naval air power to be projected anywhere where there was sea to operate; the Navy's role was seen to be control of the sea wherever US national policy demanded it.

The acrimonious debate between admirals and Air Force generals and their political supporters in Washington might have gone on indefinitely had not the Communist Democratic People's Republic of Korea chosen what it thought to be a favorable moment to attack its southern neighbor, the Republic of Korea. On Sunday 25 June 1950 six divisions of the North Korean Army crossed the 38th Parallel, taking the South Koreans by surprise and driving them back in disorder.

CHAPTER TWO
Decline and Rise

Both the United Nations and the United States reacted so swiftly that the North Koreans and their Soviet backers were taken by surprise. By 2 July the first American and British warships had been formed into Task Force 77 and were in position off the coast of Korea; and the first surface action had been fought between British units and North Korean motor torpedo boats. Next day the light fleet carrier HMS *Triumph* sent her Firefly and Seafire fighter-bombers in a strike against land targets, while the USS *Valley Forge* launched Skyraiders and Corsairs against the airfield at Pyongyang, capital of North Korea. History was made that day, for a Combat Air Patrol (CAP) of eight F-9F2 Panthers launched from the *Valley Forge* marked the first use of jet aircraft in naval combat. The two carriers continued to 'hold the ring' as the hard-pressed South Korean forces and the first wave of American reinforcements were steadily pushed southwards to the Pusan perimeter. Another

FAR LEFT: The USS *Philippine Sea* in 1950, the year in which carrier critics were discomfited.

LEFT: The USS *Princeton* (CV-37), part of the massive wartime program, leaves Philadelphia Navy Yard in January 1946 to begin her shakedown.

BOTTOM LEFT: The British *Colossus* class lacked the massive air group of the *Essex* class but were well suited to low intensity operations.

RIGHT: A Fairey Firefly, painted with 'invasion stripes' takes off from HMS *Glory* during the Suez operations in 1956.

BELOW RIGHT: Over 3000 AD Skyraiders were produced in 1945-53, and were in front line service until 1968.

carrier, the USS *Boxer*, arrived on 23 July with 145 P-51 Mustang long-range fighters, followed by the *Philippine Sea*, with a new air group. The British carrier *Triumph* was experiencing maintenance problems with her aircraft, but was able to take over CAP duties to free the *Valley Forge* air squadrons for support missions, still further proof of the flexibility of carriers in this type of conflict. Despite severe procedural problems in co-operating with Air Force controllers in close support missions, the two big carriers continued to provide close support. They flew continuous sorties for two days and then withdrew for a day to replenish fuel and stores, and to allow aircraft to be re-armed before going back into action. Two escort carriers, the *Sicily* and *Badoeng Strait*, brought two USMC Corsair squadrons into action, supporting the newly landed 1st Provisional Marine Brigade. Between 5 August and 3 September Task Force 77 and the escort carrier task group TG 96.8 flew over 3000 strikes. Their efforts, with the aid of gunfire support from battleships, cruisers and destroyers, played a major part in saving the UN forces pinned down in the Pusan perimeter and won time for massive reinforcements to turn the tide against the North Koreans.

LEFT: A USN Sikorsky HO3S-1 (S-51) helicopter lands on HMS *Triumph* during the Korean war.

BOTTOM LEFT: An F4U-1F Corsair about to launch rockets against a North Korean railway bridge.

RIGHT: A US Navy F9F-2 Panther of VF 781 takes the wire just short of the barrier on board the *Bon Homme Richard*.

BELOW: The light fleet carrier HMS *Theseus* on her way to Korea in August 1950 to relieve her sister *Triumph*.

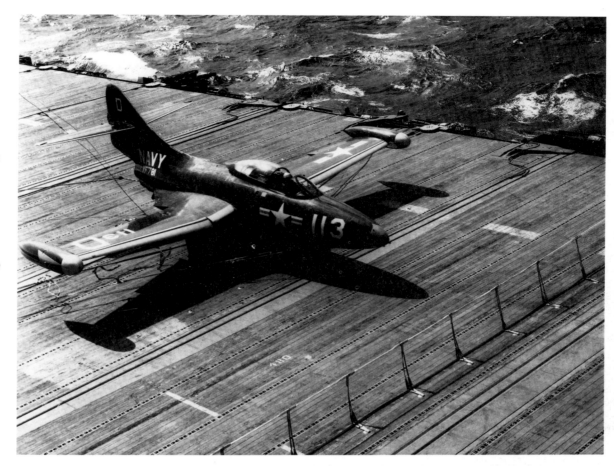

Carriers continued to play their part in the Korean War, providing cover for the Inchon amphibious landing in September 1950. The three American fleet carriers continued to form TF 77, but the British *Triumph* was replaced by her sister *Theseus,* and the USS *Leyte* replaced the *Boxer.* As land airstrips became available the strain on the carriers eased, and it became possible to divide the load. Normally the American carriers operated on the east coast, the British (and later Canadian and Australian) carriers remaining on the west coast.

It would be misleading to suggest that all this air activity took place with no North Korean or Chinese opposition. As early as August 1950 TF 77 Corsairs intercepted and shot down a Russian bomber. North Korean Yak-18s and Po.2s were no match for the allied air forces, but on 1 November 1950 the first MiG-15 jet fighters were in action, operating from Chinese bases in Manchuria, across the Yalu River.

The first all-jet engagement was fought only a week later, between four USAF F-80C Shooting Stars and four MiG-15s; one of the

LEFT: HMS *Ocean* saw action in the Korean War in 1952-53 and in the Suez Operation in 1956 as an assault carrier.

BOTTOM LEFT: A Sea Fury wrecked after hitting the flight deck barrier on board HMS *Ocean* in August 1953.

RIGHT: F9F Panthers and F4U Corsairs in the hangar of the USS *Bon Homme Richard* (CV-31) in Korean waters in November 1951.

BELOW: AD Skyraiders of the USS *Valley Forge* (CV-45) firing 5 inch rockets in North Korea in October 1950.

MiG-15s was shot down. The first Navy aircraft to destroy a MiG-15 in combat was an F-9F-2 Panther on 9 November, only a day after a USAF F-80C had downed one. In August 1952 Sea Furies operating from HMS *Ocean* were 'bounced' by MiG-15s and succeeded in shooting down one of their adversaries.

By June 1951 the Chinese intervention had been contained and both sides were glad to start negotiations for a truce, although fighting was to continue until 1953. Korea was a war which could not be won by the US and its UN allies, but it was a convincing demonstration of the Western Allies' resolve, and a timely demonstration of the way in which sea power, particularly carrier air power, could offset a massive advantage in ground forces. Even more important was the lesson for the US high command. A major confrontation with the Eastern Bloc had not resulted in the all-out nuclear war which so many pundits had predicted. Grudgingly it was admitted that carriers were ideal for dealing with 'brushfire' wars, although the USAF continued to base its strategic deterrent on

bombers and the exciting new technology of intercontinental ballistic missiles (ICBMs).

In 1959 Rep. Clarence Cannon, Chairman of the House Appropriations Committee, suggested that the Soviets had copied every US weapon system except the attack carrier (CVA) thus weakening America's defense posture. He argued that the US had dropped behind every year and the Soviet Union had correspondingly risen in military capability because the US Navy had 'ignored the missile and the submarine'. Other well-meaning critics asked why the US Navy needed carriers when it had the Polaris submarine-launched ballistic missile. The Secretary of the Navy countered such naive claims with a cogently argued statement in 1956. Locating a carrier in the vast ocean wastes, he pointed out, is an exceedingly difficult task. In six hours a carrier could be anywhere within a 100,000 square mile circle. Even when a carrier is located and positively identified, enemy aircraft must then fight their way through the carrier's own defenses, missile-armed escorts and the CAP. Secretary Thomas reminded his listeners that not a single carrier in World War II had been sunk by high-altitude bombing, and no *Essex* class carrier had been sunk by any form of attack.

The real argument against carriers was their cost. In a period of shrinking defense budgets it was inevitable that the Air Force should seek to divert funds to their own projects. The defenders of carrier air power have been able time and time again to remind their political masters that not one carrier has been lost since 1945, whereas many overseas air bases have been 'lost' by changes of government. As long as 'brushfire wars' remained a likely contingency the carriers would be cost-effective, and Nikita Khrushchev warned the West in 1961 that the Soviet Union would back 'liberation wars' as long as colonialism existed.

The next 'brushfire war' was another East-West confrontation, but on nothing like the scale of Korea. The French desire to bring their Indo-Chinese possessions back under control had sparked off a civil war, with the Chinese-backed Vietminh occupying Indo-China north of the 16th Parallel and the French controlling the south.

The old carrier *Béarn* was too slow for combat duty but she served as a transport, taking reinforcements from Saigon to Haiphong in February 1946. After fierce fighting the French managed to reoccupy Haiphong and forced the Chinese to withdraw, but it was clear that pacification would mean a long and bloody war.

The first operational carrier to reach Indo-China was the ex-RN escort carrier *Dixmude*, which arrived in March 1947 with a squadron of SBD-5 Dauntless divebombers and a ferry cargo of aircraft for the French Air Force. Although poorly equipped for sustained operations she was in action only ten days after her arrival, her divebombers flying support missions against Vietminh positions and providing cover for amphibious landings. After a brief refit the little CVE returned to Indo-China in October. Her finest achievement was a three-week mission supporting a paratroop assault in the Tonkin area, during which her single squadron flew over 200 sorties and dropped 65 tons of bombs and rockets.

The *Dixmude* continued to operate in Indo-Chinese waters until 1948 but reinforcements were on the way. The British had transferred a new 14,000-ton light fleet carrier, the *Arromanches*, which took over the CVE's divebombers and Seafire fighter-bombers. But the age and obsolescence of these aircraft hampered air operations severely, and the two carriers were withdrawn in late 1949/early 1950 to await the delivery of 'modern' aircraft from the United States. These were SB-2C Helldivers and F-6F Hellcat fighters, hardly in their prime but they revitalized French carrier air power in the conflict. When the *Arromanches* returned to the battle zone she was able to fly one and a half times as many sorties.

In June 1951 the US Navy transferred the CVL *Langley*, which was renamed *Lafayette* in honor of previous Franco-American military co-operation. Two years later another CVL, the USS *Belleau Wood*, was transferred and became the *Bois Belleau*. But the war was not going well. Chinese support for the Vietminh enhanced their fighting abilities, enabling them to dominate the mountain regions and the forests.

To counter this turn of events the French High Command launched Operation 'Castor', the seizure of Dien Bien Phu, a valley controlling the Communist supply-route into Laos. The end of the Korean War enabled the Chinese to divert enormous quantities of munitions and other supplies to north Indo-China, and the French severely underestimated the Vietminh's ability to move supplies. Equally disastrous was French over-estimation of their own ability to function at the end of a 170-mile supply-line, and the result was tragedy for the French forces.

The French Navy pilots flew over 1200 sorties during the five-and-a-half month siege of Dien Bien Phu, losing many aircraft in their desperate efforts to bring help to the beleaguered garrison. But it was all too late, even with US aid. At one stage a large-scale American strike was planned but no agreement could be reached. Dien Bien Phu fell on 7 May 1954 and with it died any hope of winning the political battle.

The Suez operation of 1956 brought the

RIGHT: Obsolescent F6F Hellcat fighters were used by the French Navy in Indochina.

BOTTOM RIGHT: Seafire fighters were equipped with Rocket Assisted Take Off (RATO) gear to improve payload.

ABOVE: The huge Westland S.4 Wyvern propeller-engined strike fighter had only a short service life.

LEFT: A Seahawk of 802 Sqn returned to HMS *Albion* with damage to her long-range fuel tank from Egyptian ground fire.

RIGHT: The De Havilland Sea Venom two seat strike fighter was in Fleet Air Arm service from 1953 to 1959.

British and French into direct conflict with the United States, who correctly foresaw the risk of alienating Arab opinion if the two allies colluded with Israel in an attack on Egypt. The British hoped to bring the Suez Canal back under their control, while the French hoped to punish Egypt for her support for Algerian independence. But even though the political consequences of the Anglo-French intervention proved disastrous, the carrier operations were one of the few redeeming features of the military events which ensued.

The British were able to deploy the new large carrier *Eagle* and two smaller carriers, the *Albion* and *Bulwark,* while the French provided two light fleet carriers, the *Arromanches* and *Lafayette*. The British carriers operated the Sea Venom, the RN's first jet all-weather fighter, the Sea Hawk jet fighter, the propeller-driven Wyvern strike aircraft and the AD-4W Avenger airborne early warning aircraft. The French operated F-4U-7 Corsairs and TBM-3S and -3W Avenger torpedo-bombers. In addition the RN pressed two light fleet carriers, the *Ocean* and *Theseus,*

ABOVE: The Westland Whirlwind HAR.9 was derived from the Sikorsky S-55 and served for many years on search and rescue (SAR) duties.

TOP RIGHT: The Wessex HAS.1, developed from the Sikorsky S-58, replaced the Whirlwind and is seen on the deck of an LPD.

BOTTOM RIGHT: RAF Westland Whirlwind HAR.10s landing on HMS *Eagle* during a 1965 exercise in the South China Sea.

into service as troop transports to rush reinforcements to the Mediterranean, and then reconverted them to helicopter assault ships. Within four days the two ships were back at sea, practising the radically different routines needed to put combat troops ashore.

Hostilities against Egypt began on the night of 31 October, when RAF bombers from Cyprus and Malta attacked airfield targets, and at dawn naval aircraft followed up with attacks on military targets in the Nile Delta. Antiaircraft fire was light and there was no opposition from the Russian-supplied MiG-15 fighters of the Egyptian Air Force. Several naval targets were sunk, including motor torpedo boats, and by midday on 2 November it was clear that the Anglo-French air forces had won supremacy.

Despite the air victory the assault did not take place until 5 November, when British and French paratroops dropped on Port Said. Next day the amphibious assault began, giving the *Ocean* and *Theseus* their cue for flying in Royal Marine commandos in the world's first vertical assault. Despite the poor capacity of the Whirlwinds and Sycamores it proved possible to land 415 commandos and 23 tons of ammunition and equipment in 89 minutes. Despite heavy ground fire the commandos were able to seize their objective with only light casualties.

The gains won by the daring of the paratroops and the commandos were frittered away, and the Anglo-French forces failed to capture the Canal. The lethargic planning and lack of coherent political objectives encouraged world-wide hostility, and the British and French were forced into an ignominious withdrawal. What had been proved

beyond argument, however, was once again the aircraft carrier's indispensable role in supporting such operations.

For both these conflicts, the aircraft, weapons and tactics were largely the same as in World War II. The lessons learned were invaluable in recasting US naval aviation plans, but of course the most crucial outcome of Korea was the reversal of the 1949 defeat of the nuclear land bomber lobby. Another less tangible result was the slow dawning of understanding among political and military leaders that there was a 'limited' war which need not result in a nuclear holocaust. Of course it could also be argued by the nuclear planners and strategic bombing advocates that Korea had taught the Communist Bloc that victory over the West was possible *only* through nuclear superiority.

The Suez debacle had merely exacerbated tension in the Middle East, and in April 1957 the Sixth Fleet was ordered to cruise in the Eastern Mediterranean as a visible sign of support for King Hussein of Jordan. The Jordanian king had only just put down an Egyptian and Syrian inspired mutiny in his army.

In May the following year came the first sign of trouble in the Lebanon, with a request from the Lebanese government for assistance. Then in July Arab nationalists seized power in neighboring Iraq, assassinating the King and his pro-Western prime minister. In response to a specific request from President Chamoun the US Marines were put ashore near Beirut on 15 July. The whole operation looked somewhat ridiculous when it emerged that the President's appeal for help was based on an incorrect intelligence assessment, and the Lebanon landing was caricatured as 'an invasion of American pressmen accompanied by their bodyguards'. However, the verdict of history must be that the landing served its political purpose; yet again the US government had shown its willingness to act quickly in support of allies and friendly nations.

The resources of the US Navy were so vast that it proved possible to deal with another, much more serious crisis on the other side of the world, without affecting the Lebanon operations. In August that year the Communist Chinese started a bombardment of the Nationalist (Taiwan) Chinese islands of Little and Big Quemoy and Matsu, near Amoy. The islands were garrisoned by 85,000 Nationalist troops, and were perilously close to the Communist-controlled mainland. Although ownership of the offshore islands was in dispute and the US was wary of being drawn into another conflict with Communist China, the Seventh Fleet was put on alert to honor the US government's promise to protect the Nationalists from mainland aggression. The force mustered included six carriers, the

Hancock, Shangri-la, Lexington, Princeton, Midway and *Essex,* and it proved possible to escort resupply convoys to the beleaguered islands without precipitating a shooting war with the Communists. The show of strength served its purpose; the artillery bombardments were lifted and the islands remain under Nationalist control to this day.

The British had restructured their forces after Suez to improve their effectiveness in dealing with such small conflicts, working on the sound principle that swift action prevents minor crises from developing into full-scale wars. The Royal Navy's contribution was to convert two carriers, HMS *Albion* and HMS *Bulwark,* to 'commando' carriers, removing their arrester wires and catapults and equipping them to operate only assault helicopters. Each carrier accommodated 600 Royal Marine commando troops and their vehicles. The first to be completed was the *Bulwark* in January 1960 and the *Albion* rejoined the fleet in August the following year.

The new concept was to be put to the test almost immediately. In June the military ruler of Iraq, Colonel Kassem, demanded the oilfields of neighboring Kuwait. His armed forces almost outnumbered the entire population of Kuwait, and his Soviet-supplied weaponry seemed to promise a walkover. For the British it would have been a huge embarrassment, for Kuwait was a former protectorate and had a guarantee against external aggression. The overrunning of the small sheikhdom would have deprived the West of oil, and might easily have embroiled the remaining independent Gulf States in a ruinous war. The problem for Kuwait was that outside aid, such as that offered by Britain

and friendly Arab states, might not arrive before the Iraqis invaded. Only sea power could offer the speed of response needed, without the need to push the Kuwaitis into asking for a landing. The commando carrier *Bulwark* was ordered to leave Karachi and the fleet carrier *Victorious* was ordered to sail from the South China Sea to the Gulf.

On 30 June the Sheikh of Kuwait formally requested military assistance from the British and Saudi governments, and HMS *Bulwark* was ordered to land her marines next day. As HMS *Victorious* was too far away to provide air cover there was a considerable risk from Iraqi naval and air force

units. Boldness paid off, however, and the 16 Whirlwind helicopters achieved a textbook landing on the airport in Kuwait. A week later Colonel Kassem announced that the Iraqi claim was only 'formal' and would not be backed up by military action.

The second commando carrier HMS *Albion* also found useful employment. While steaming through the Indian Ocean on her first commission she received orders to help the Sultanate of Brunei put down a rebellion. The insurrection was dealt with promptly but many of the rebels had taken refuge in the jungle. With the encouragement of the Indonesians the insurgents started to infiltrate back into Borneo, and the *Albion*'s helicopters were used to patrol the border.

The border insurgency gradually drifted into full confrontation, with Indonesia committing its forces to a hit-and-run war in

Borneo, in the hope of destabilizing newly independent Malaysia. Fortunately the battle for hearts and minds among the inhabitants of Borneo, particularly the Ibans, was never lost, and incursions by Indonesian regulars and irregulars were contained by British and Malaysian troops until President Sukarno was removed from power by the Indonesian military in 1965. It nevertheless forced the British to maintain two fleet carriers east of Suez and one commando carrier.

While this confrontation was in progress, civil war broke out in the Yemen. This could be dealt with by ground forces in Aden but a mutiny in the Tanganyikan Army in January 1964 required a very rapid response. The carrier HMS *Centaur* embarked Royal Marine commandos and equipment at Aden in less than a day (20 January) and was in position off Dar-es-Salaam four days later.

ABOVE: The new HMS *Ark Royal* arrives in New York in June 1957. Although she never saw action in 21 years of service she kept the Fleet Air Arm alive.

RIGHT: The commando carrier HMS *Albion* and her half-sister *Hermes* (background) in Malta in the 1960s.

The speed of the landing took the mutineers by surprise and they surrendered after putting up only light resistance, but further operations were necessary against up-country mutineers before the mutiny was suppressed. In retrospect it appeared no more than a local police action but *Centaur's* marines had achieved their success in less than 24 hours and had thereby avoided bloodshed and unrest in a newly independent country.

It might be thought that this series of successful carrier operations would have ensured the survival of British carrier air power, but appearances were misleading. The Royal Navy's carriers lacked aircraft capacity; the increasing size of high-performance aircraft meant that in the 1960s the five British fleet carriers could only muster 145 fixed-wing aircraft and 40 helicopters between them. What was needed was something akin to the US Navy's supercarriers (see next chapter) and in July 1963 an official announcement confirmed that a new 50,000 ton-plus carrier would be ordered as a replacement for *Ark Royal* and *Victorious,* leaving the modernized *Eagle* and the smaller *Hermes* to make up a striking force of three carriers that would last at least until the end of the 1970s. Construction of *CVA.01,* as the new carrier was designated, was to begin in 1966, with commissioning in 1972, and long-term plans allowed for *CVA.02* to replace *Eagle* and *Hermes.*

In the ensuing inter-service battle for scarce funds the Royal Air Force dusted off some of the arguments which had already been discarded in the United States a decade earlier. Carriers were vulnerable to intercontinental ballistic missiles, the Russians hadn't built any carriers, and land-based bombers were more effective.

The upshot was that *CVA.01* was canceled in 1966, a near-mortal blow for the Royal Navy. The *Victorious* was retired early, and the recently modernized *Eagle* was earmarked for early retirement. Her unmodernized sister *Ark Royal* was also to retire in 1972 but a series of overseas crises forced the government to rescind the decision. The *Ark* ran on until 1978, becoming more decrepit as the years went by, but winning a place in public affection which had been previously denied her.

Other navies were finding the cost of carriers prohibitive. The Royal Netherlands Navy was forced to sell the *Karel Doorman* (ex-HMS *Venerable*) to Argentina in 1968 without a replacement. The Canadian Navy paid off the *Bonaventure* in 1970, but the Australian Navy managed to keep the *Melbourne* (ex-HMS *Majestic*) running to 1982. By 1990 the only small navies still operating carriers are Argentina, Brazil and India.

Although never completed the *United States* (CVA-58) had considerable influence over subsequent carrier designs. She had been designed originally to operate AJ-1 Savage twin-engined heavy strategic (nuclear) bombers, although the design was subsequently amended to allow for non-strategic roles. On a standard displacement of some 66,000 tons she would have been driven at a speed of 33 knots by four-shaft steam turbines. Major innovations were the abandonment of the island superstructure and the positioning of two additional catapults in the 'waist'. With four deck-edge lifts the carrier would have been able to launch four aircraft simultaneously, two from the forward catapults and one on either side amidships. However the arrester wires were still aligned fore and aft, so she was not an angled-deck carrier in the true sense and could not recover and launch aircraft simultaneously.

The *United States* class (four were planned) were originally intended to operate with the bombers stowed on deck, because the aircraft would be too big to strike down into the hangar. Indeed, early proposals showed no hangar at all, but at later stages in the design the hangar was reintroduced to provide accommodation for the escorting fighters. The catapults would have been a new cylindrical type using internal combustion.

It seems strange to have reverted to a flush deck layout with a Japanese-style horizontal uptake at the edge of the flight deck, after all the years of building successful island carriers. The designers seem to have admitted that the problems of smoke dispersal would prove intractable, and it seemed likely that the later ships of the class would be nuclear powered, thereby eliminating the problem.

After the convincing demonstration of carrier air power in the Korean War there was no opposition to the idea of building new carriers. The first pair of 'supercarriers' was laid down in 1952, slightly smaller than the defunct *United States* but using the same type of four-shaft steam powerplant. Initially they were to have the same flush deck arrangement but during the design phase the island superstructure was introduced once more. This time the waist catapults were both positioned on the port side.

Much thought had gone into the design of the *Forrestal* class (CVA-59/62). They were the first CVAs built specifically to operate jet aircraft, reflected in the enormous capacity for aviation fuel and ordnance. As built the *Forrestal* could store 750,000 gallons of avgas and 789,000 gallons of JP-5, as compared to 500,000 gallons of avgas planned for the *United States* and 365,000 gallons for the *Midway* class. This was a massive

increase but every other aspect of the *Forrestal* was equally 'super': 70 per cent more fuel oil than a modernized *Essex* class, 300 per cent more aviation fuel, 154 per cent more aviation ordnance, and 15 per cent more nuclear weapons for the strategic role.

Although many feared that jet aircraft would be incompatible with carriers, many ideas and inventions were tried, and some succeeded brilliantly. The British, operating smaller carriers, anticipated the 'squeeze' and led the search for new techniques. One idea was to save fuel and reduce the risk from high-speed landings by eliminating the wheeled undercarriage. A conference at the Royal Aircraft Establishment at Farnborough in 1945 led to the conversion of HMS *Warrior* in 1948 to allow Sea Vampires to land on a flexible carpet rigged on her flight deck.

CHAPTER THREE

New Technology and Techniques

Over 200 landings made between November 1948 and May 1949 proved that undercarriageless aircraft could land safely on the flexible deck, and could also achieve 4-5% weight reduction, even with existing airframes. Given the very short endurance of early jets this meant 45 minutes more flying time or a slight increase in speed. What killed the idea was the inevitable consequence that undercarriageless aircraft would need special landing fields wherever they operated. Even the cost of developing a new range of aircraft for the task would have been too expensive, let alone the re-equipping of naval air stations and overseas airfields with special landing arrangements. Since 1917 one of the most valued characteristics of naval aircraft has been their ability to fly ashore if for any reason they cannot return to their carrier. The flexible deck concept would have put the clock back to 1915 in terms of operational flexibility, whatever merits it had as a landing aid.

LEFT: Loading bombs on to an F4U Corsair on board the USS *Boxer* (CVC-21) during the Korean War. A new 'brushfire war' strategy was beginning to unfold, an alternative to the assumption that all-out nuclear war was inescapable.

ABOVE: The Griffon-engined Seafire served against Communist guerrillas in Malaya and for a time in the Korean War.

BELOW: The Vampire F.1 was developed into the Sea Vampire when it proved capable of landing on a carrier in 1945.

The next British idea sounded more prosaic but proved to be a giant step forward in carrier design. Captain Dennis Campbell RN proposed in 1951 that the landing-on deck should be offset 10deg to port. This would permit an aircraft which missed an arrester wire to accelerate clear and go around again, avoiding the risk of crashing into the barrier or the deck park. Another important benefit is the ability to launch aircraft from the forward catapults while simultaneously recovering aircraft on the angled deck; previously launching had to wait until landing operations were over, because of the con-

gested 'deck park' ahead of the crash barrier.

In February 1952 the light fleet carrier *Triumph* was given a painted deck layout, with some obstructions removed from the port side. A short while later the US Navy (which followed the *Warrior* trials with great interest) painted a similar layout on the deck of the USS *Midway*. Touch-and-go landings were successful in both carriers, and in September that year the *Essex* class *Antietam* was taken in hand for a full conversion. When she emerged three months later her arrester wires and crash barriers had been realigned to conform to an 8deg angled deck on the port side, with the port aircraft lift locking at flight deck level to form an extension. Tests were a great success, with barrier crashes falling sharply, and the angled deck was immediately adopted by carrier operating navies. During completion HMS *Ark Royal* was given a 5½deg angle, and it was appropriate that her first captain should be Dennis Campbell, who had proposed the idea. In one form or another the angled deck is still in use in all carriers.

British innovation did not end there. The rising weight of aircraft was as much of a headache to carrier designers and naval aviators as their landing speeds. Using steam from the ship's boilers it was possible to drive a pair of pistons in a slotted cylinder with more controlled force than existing hydraulic catapults. In 1950-51 the maintenance carrier HMS *Perseus* was refitted with a steel structure at the forward end of her flight deck, carrying the prototype Mitchell steam catapult.

Once again the trials were a brilliant

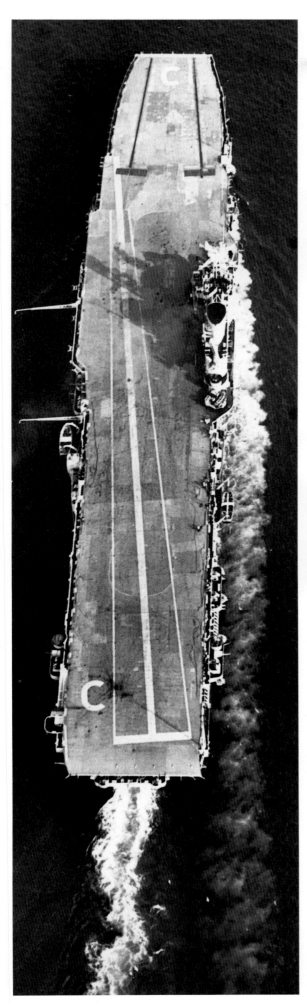

success, and the US Navy immediately adopted the idea. Not content with two successes the British went on to tackle the remaining problem of how to control landing approach. Both the USN and RN had previously employed a Landing Signal Officer (LSO) or 'batsman' to tell the pilot if he was correctly aligned for landing, and when to cut his engine. Jet aircraft were, however, proving too fast for the LSO's reactions; nor could turbojet engines react fast enough to throttle changes.

A Royal Navy pilot on exchange with the US Navy concluded that if the pilot could see a mirror image of his aircraft he could make his own adjustments faster and with more safety. Legend has it that the first trial was done with a secretary's mirror and lipstick, enabling the officer to put his chin down on the desk. Whatever the truth of the story the mirror landing sight was developed successfully, and all carriers use derivatives. A light positioned near the end of the flight deck shone forward into a mirror, creating a 'meatball' image visible to the pilot. If he was

ABOVE: HMS *Bulwark* shows off her interim 5¾° angled deck after commissioning in November 1954.

LEFT: The *Bulwark*'s sister *Centaur* joined the fleet in 1953. Her higher speed and greater aircraft capacity made her more efficient than the light fleet carriers.

on the correct glidepath the light would be in the center of the mirror – too high or too low, and the light would vary accordingly. The first trials took place aboard HMS *Albion*, followed by trials in the USS *Bennington* in 1955. Today's US carriers use a much more advanced derivative, with fresnel lenses and lamps replacing the mirror and light, but the principle remains the same.

The ultimate point of all these improvements is to maximize the efficiency of aircraft operations. Current practice in the US Navy is to vary between the 'Alfa strike', launching the maximum number of aircraft as close together as possible, and the 'Flex-Deck' mode, launching a continuous stream of aircraft. An 'Alfa strike' puts the maximum number of aircraft over the target and thereby reduces the risk of losses. But while the strike is being launched the carrier is at her most vulnerable, with the flight deck crowded with aircraft and ordnance. The 'Flex-Deck' concept limits that risk but the aircraft will be more vulnerable as they hit the target area at five- or ten-minute intervals.

The US Navy was luckier than the Royal Navy in having the *Essex* class, but the three British inventions were a great help in adapting these fine wartime ships to the modern age. Work on one hull, the USS *Oriskany* (CV-34), had been suspended at the end of World War II, and she was completed to a drastically uprated design known as SCB-27A. She emerged in 1950 looking very different from the original *Essex* class, with a small island incorporating a raked funnel. Less obvious were the improvements to the

flight deck; suppressing deck guns left more area clear for flying, and two high-capacity H-8 catapults were provided at the forward end. To improve aircrew access to the flight deck an escalator was provided outboard of the island, connecting new ready rooms. The flight deck was also strengthened to compensate for heavier naval aircraft.

Eight more carriers were given the SCB-27A modernization, the *Essex, Wasp, Kearsage, Lake Champlain, Bennington, Yorktown, Randolph* and *Hornet*. Two badly damaged veterans, the *Bunker Hill* and the *Franklin*, were kept in reserve, but the converted ships were so successful that six more were selected for modernization. The SCB-27C conversion broadly followed the lines of SCB-27A but had the first steam catapults as well as strengthened arresting gear. In time both groups received steam catapults and angled decks.

By the time the *Forrestal* class started to enter service a new generation of carrier aircraft was available. There were improved models of the F-2H Banshee and the F-9F-6 Cougar was the first swept-wing fighter to become operational. Even more advanced was the F-7U Cutlass, a tailless twin-engined single-seat fighter capable of Mach 1 flight. After re-engining the F-7U-3 became a very potent carrier fighter but it proved a difficult machine to fly and was never popular with the pilots. After numerous accidents the Cutlass was withdrawn in 1957, only three years after the last deliveries had been made to the fleet.

The first aircraft to fly from the *Forrestal*

LEFT: Grumman F9F-6 and -8 Cougars on board the super carrier USS *Saratoga* (CVA-60).

BOTTOM LEFT: The De Havilland DH.110, later named the Sea Vixen, lands on HMS *Albion* in 1954.

BELOW: The McDonnell F2H Banshee could climb 7380ft per minute to a height of 48,500ft, setting new performance standards.

was the FJ-3 Fury, which was developed from the land-based F-86 Sabre. A new ground-attack weapon was also coming into service, the Bullpup Mach 2 missile which gave aircraft a three-mile standoff range. Space does not permit an inventory of US Navy aircraft of the period, but all were high-performance aircraft which matched the performance of land-based contemporaries. The F-4D Skyray, for example, was the USN's first delta-wing fighter and held the world air speed record in 1953. The F-3H1 Demon briefly took the altitude record by reaching 10,000 feet in 71 seconds, only to be beaten a month later by the F-4D reaching 10,000 feet in 56 seconds.

Another generation of carrier aircraft began to emerge in the late 1950s, starting with the F-8U Crusader, an interceptor which is still flying over 30 years later. By 1960 more than half of the USN's 30 carrier fighter squadrons and most of the USMC fighter squadrons had been re-equipped with the Crusader.

The attack squadrons were also being modernized, with the A-3D Skywarrior and the A-4D Skyhawk. The Skywarrior, the first jet carrier-based attack aircraft, was also the largest so far. It had a normal weight of 70,000 pounds, and a speed of Mach 0.9 at 10,000 feet. The A-3D squadrons were deployed aboard the *Midway* and *Forrestal* classes, providing the US Navy with an all-weather nuclear strike capability by day or by night. They replaced the piston-jet AJ-1 Savages, and performed valiant service in Vietnam.

Much better known, because it is still flying in the 1990s, is the A-4D Skyhawk. Known as 'Heinemann's Hot Rod' from the chief designer of the Douglas Aircraft Company, the Skyhawk weighed only 15,000 pounds loaded but could take off at 22,000 pounds. It was small enough to dispense with folding wings, yet could deliver a tactical nuclear weapon. It was also a comparatively simple aircraft, with comparatively little in the way of avionics or even navigation equipment. Refinements were added as the years passed but the Skyhawk remained a rugged and capable aircraft which continued to prove itself in combat. During the Falklands conflict in 1982 much of the damage inflicted on British ships was done by Argentine Navy A-4Q Skyhawks flying from land bases.

Although the British aircraft industry could never hope to match the achievements of the American industry, the Fleet Air Arm also made big strides during this period. The Sea Vixen all-weather fighter replaced the Sea Venom from 1959, and was the first British carrier aircraft armed with air-to-air missiles. The Scimitar was the new day fighter/strike aircraft, the first to be capable

TOP LEFT: The Grumman F9F-8T Cougar was the US Navy's first swept wing trainer. It made its maiden flight in 1956.

CENTER LEFT: The unusual Chance Vought F7U Cutlass was a tailless single seat fighter. It proved temperamental and was withdrawn in 1957.

BOTTOM LEFT: A Cougar (foreground) on the catapult, and a Skyray, Fury and Demon parked on the foredeck of the USS *Forrestal* (CVA-59).

ABOVE: The F3H-1N Demon first flew from the USS *Coral Sea* (CVCA-43) in 1955.

RIGHT: In 1953 the delta winged Douglas F4D Skyray was the first carrier aircraft to capture the world speed record.

of supersonic flight in a shallow dive. But a far more advanced aircraft was under development. The Blackburn NA.39 Buccaneer was the first in the world specifically designed to carry out low-level high-speed bombing. Still in service with the RAF (which took over FAA Buccaneers in 1978) this bomber can fly under radar cover but the airframe is rugged enough to cope with the extreme buffeting and turbulence at low altitudes.

The other great innovation in carrier design was nuclear propulsion. The USS *Enterprise* (CVAN-65), when she appeared in 1961,

was unique, capable of steaming almost indefinitely at 32 knots, yet requiring virtually no internal volume for oil fuel. This permitted more aviation fuel to be carried, hence a bigger air group. The island could be configured for maximum efficiency, both for personnel and for electronics, and the absence of funnel smoke greatly simplified the task of landing aircraft.

Although the 'billboard' plan radar arrays on the square sides of the island superstructure were not a great success the *Enterprise* proved very successful, and the Service Life Extension Program (SLEP) recently

TOP: A photographic reconnaissance F8U-1P Crusader from VFP 62 operating from the USS *Forrestal* (CXV-59) in the Atlantic.

ABOVE: The Douglas A3D Skywarrior nuclear bomber was the largest carrier aircraft yet developed.

approved by Congress should give her another 25 years of operational life.

Aircraft carrier armaments have changed. At the end of World War II massive light and medium caliber guns were obligatory, but as the need for more deck space and topweight margins were reduced by radars, guns became less important. The *Forrestals*, for example, started with eight single 5 inch Mk 42 guns in four sponsons, but it was soon found that the forward sponsons threw up too much spray, so the guns and sponsons were removed. Then the aft guns were replaced by Sea Sparrow missile launchers.

The British carriers *Eagle* and *Ark Royal* also started out with heavy gun batteries, eight twin 4.5 inch guns in four sponsons,

TOP: A Blackburn Buccaneer S.2 low level bomber carrying out trials aboard HMS *Hermes* in 1964.

CENTER: A Sea Vixen FAW.2 of 892 Squadron spotted on the catapult on board HMS *Hermes*.

RIGHT: The A4D-1 Skyhawk makes its first deck landing in September 1955. 'Heinemann's Hot Rod' was the smallest carrier aircraft capable of lifting a nuclear weapon.

but these were progressively removed to reduce weight and to make way for additional flight deck area. HMS *Eagle* was rearmed with six quadruple Seacat missile launchers, but her half-sister *Ark Royal,* although fitted to receive four Seacat systems, never received them.

Armor also became less important, although the *Midways* were the first US carriers to have armored decks. In general carriers operated by smaller navies followed American and British practice, adopting the angled deck, mirror landing sight and steam catapult from the RN, but like the RN largely following US Navy practice in flight deck procedures.

The French Navy continued to operate the ex-RN *Arromanches* until 1962, when she became a combined helicopter assault and training carrier. At about the same time the old CVLs *Lafayette* and *Bois Belleau* were returned to the US Navy, when their replacements were ready.

The *Clemenceau* and *Foch* were the outcome of studies in progress since the late 1940s, and emerged as 33,000-tonne ships with all the postwar improvements. Both ships have undergone constant upgrades and improvements since the early 1960s, when they joined the fleet. They became the backbone of the *Aeronavale*'s strength at sea, operating 60 aircraft originally but reducing to 40 as size of aircraft rose. In 1963 42 F-8E Crusaders were ordered from the United States to give the two carriers effective modern fighters, but a new French strike aircraft, the Etendard IV, was designed to operate from the two ships.

Although the Royal Navy had designed its *Colossus* class light fleet carriers as utility ships they proved highly successful in the postwar world. In addition to the *Arromanches* (ex-HMS *Colossus*) the Dutch were given HMS *Venerable,* which became HNlMS *Karel Doorman,* the Canadians received first HMS *Warrior* (until 1948), then HMS *Magnificent* (until 1957) and finally the incomplete hull of HMS *Powerful*. As HMCS *Bonaven-*

ABOVE: A French Navy F-8E (FN) Crusader armed with the Matra R 530 air to air missile.

LEFT: HMS *Bulwark* anchored off Tromso in Norway in 1981 after landing 42 Royal Marine Commando, using HAS.2 Sea King, HC.4 Commando and Wessex 5 helicopters.

ture she incorporated all the latest improvements, but was equipped with USN pattern radars and guns.

Australia was given HMAS *Sydney* (ex-HMS *Terrible*) in 1948 and then lent HMS *Vengeance* from 1952 until 1955, as a stopgap until the *Melbourne* (ex-HMS *Majestic*) was ready. The *Sydney* was a victim of defense cuts, and was reduced to a training carrier and then a transport from 1954, but the *Melbourne* remained operational until 1982. In 1956 Brazil bought HMS *Vengeance* and renamed her *Minas Gerais.* The last of the light fleet carriers to be sold was the incomplete *Hercules,* which underwent four years of modernization at Harland & Wolff's shipyard and emerged as the Indian Navy's *Vikrant.* The only remaining country to operate one of this remarkable class of carriers was Argentina, which bought the *Karel Doorman* from the Netherlands Navy in 1968, renaming her *Veinticinco de Mayo* (25 May – Independence Day).

The idea of using rotary-wing aircraft at sea was pioneered by both sides in World War II. The U-boat arm of the *Kriegsmarine* tested the Focke Angelis Fa-300 *Bachsteize,* a single-seat observation kite towed behind a submarine. Some 200 Fa-300s were put into production but very few saw operational service.

Early in 1944 a Sikorsky YR-4B underwent trials aboard a British merchant ship in the Atlantic, with a view to establishing the value of helicopters in anti-submarine warfare. The idea was ahead of its time; the YR-4B was underpowered for the task and the deck was too small.

Postwar the helicopter became popular as a 'plane guard' for carriers flying off and recovering aircraft, but it was not until the 1960s that its value as a hunter of submarines became established. Sensors were beginning to outstrip the range of ship-mounted anti-submarine weapons, and the helicopter offered an alternative, flying out to the point of detection to release a depth-charge or homing torpedo.

The two leading exponents of anti-submarine warfare (ASW), the Americans and the British, realized that there had to be a difference between 'light' and 'heavy' helicopters. The former was merely a weapon delivery vehicle, the latter could be developed as a platform for sensors as well as weapons. The Sikorsky S-55 was equipped with a 'dunking' sonar and winch, allowing it to localize and attack targets already located by ships' sonars.

The SH-3 Sea King proved even better, for it could lift a respectable quantity of weapons and still remain airborne for some hours. The Royal Navy went a step further, developing the Sea King HAS.2 into a 'flying frigate' with the ability to process sonar data on board. The Sea King has the ability to acquire and prosecute contacts without external assistance if necessary, a philosophy which is carried over to the new Anglo-Italian Merlin EH.101.

During the 1950s the US Navy designated the old *Enterprise* and the unmodernized *Essex* class carriers as support carriers (CVS). The active ships were equipped with helicopters and ASW aircraft, HSLs, HUP-2s and S-2F Trackers. The successful British use of helicopter assault at Suez has already been mentioned, but the technique was first developed by the US Marine Corps. The former escort carrier *Thetis Bay* (CVE-90) was taken in hand in 1955 and given accommodation for 1000 marines, with redesigned lifts to move vehicles and equipment to the flight deck.

The success of the *Thetis Bay* (redesignated CVHA-1) led to orders for new purpose-built ships, the seven *Iwo Jima* (LPH-2) class. On a displacement of 11,000 tons they combine some of the attributes of escort carriers and light fleet carriers, and can operate STOVL aircraft. As an interim measure three unmodernized *Essex* class, the *Boxer*, *Princeton* and *Valley Forge*, were reclassified as LPH-4/5 and -8 from the beginning of 1959, and the *Tarawa* operated US Marine Corps helicopters on a temporary basis.

The Royal Navy, as we have seen, embraced the concept of helicopter assault, and developed its own solution to the demands of seaborne ASW. To maximize the number of strike aircraft and fighters which could be embarked in *CVA.01* a parallel design was drawn up for a pure helicopter carrier. When the big carrier project was canceled in 1966 this concept evolved into the 'through deck cruiser', which eventually became the *Invincible* class.

At first it was assumed that the *Invincibles* would operate only HAS.2 Sea Kings, but the RN gradually won the political battle to get STOVL aircraft, and after the *Invincible* was launched, the first orders were placed for the FRS.1 Sea Harrier. What made the Harrier

and its maritime Sea Harrier variant unique was its vectored thrust Pegasus turbofan engine, which enables the aircraft to hover in flight and land like a helicopter. Although originally known as Vertical Take Off and Landing (VTOL) aircraft, Harrier type aircraft are more correctly known as Short Take Off and Vertical Landing (STOVL). Vertical takeoff is feasible but it uses up large amounts of fuel and so aircraft normally make a rolling takeoff.

The unusual combination of forward and vertical lift in STOVL aircraft led to a remarkable innovation. An engineer officer in the old fixed-wing carrier *Ark Royal* designed a 'ski jump' or flight deck ramp. The Sea Harrier merely rolls forward and up the ramp, thereby saving a large amount of fuel. This simple device, requiring no more than a light structural addition to the forward end of the flight deck, means that an aircraft can either have a longer range, or a heavier payload depending on the mission.

As a STOVL aircraft makes comparatively little impact on takeoff and landing, a STOVL carrier can dispense with the heavy catapult and arresting gear and their supporting structures. The *Invincible* class are fairly spacious, accommodating eight Sea Harriers and a dozen Sea Kings, yet displacing only 19,000 tons. Even the 11,000-ton *Iwo Jima* class in the US Navy can operate four of the US Marine Corps' AV-8A version of the land Harrier, and the big *Tarawa* class LHAs have operated 22 AV-8As on occasion.

RIGHT: A British Aerospace FRS.1 Sea Harrier takes off over the 'ski jump' of a Royal Navy *Invincible* class carrier. Sea King helicopters are parked to the right of the ramp.

BELOW: HMS *Invincible*, first of three 'through deck cruisers' making a tight turn to starboard during an exercise off Norway. She and her sisters are designed to operate STOVL aircraft and anti-submarine helicopters.

The end of the war between France and the Vietminh left Indo-China partitioned into North and South Vietnam, separated by a Demilitarized Zone (DMZ) along the 17th Parallel. As in Korea the imposed partition merely postponed the day when the Communist North, led by Ho Chi Minh, would try to reunify the country.

The United States, although providing massive military aid to the French, had managed to avoid direct involvement. An air strike by the Seventh Fleet's carriers had been considered as a last despairing effort to prevent the fall of Dien Bien Phu, but had been overruled at the last minute because it was held to be against American interests to get involved in a war on the Asian mainland. Yet only four years later the numbers of American military advisers to South Vietnam were rising steadily. Direct American involvement had started in 1956, first with the humanitarian task of resettling refugees in the South, and then the training of a new Army of the Republic of Vietnam (ARVN).

It was soon clear that the Communists in Hanoi were determined to overthrow the South Vietnamese government, and Communist insurgents known as the Viet Cong started a compaign of sabotage, intimidation and murder. Although by 1964 a number of US military personnel had been killed in action and there were some 23,000 of them in the country, the US Navy's carriers had been limited to flying photographic reconnaissance missions.

All this was to change after an attack by North Vietnamese motor torpedo boats in August 1964 on a destroyer of the Seventh Fleet patroling in the Gulf of Tonkin. Four F-8E Crusaders from the carrier *Ticonderoga* on patrol in the area were ordered to attack the MTBs; after several strafing runs with rockets and 20mm gunfire one MTB was sunk. The North Vietnamese attack came in fact after a South Vietnamese naval raid on their territory, and the USS *Maddox* was probably mistaken for a South Vietnamese warship.

Two nights later the *Maddox* and another destroyer, the *Turner Joy*, opened fire on what they took to be hostile contacts, and although there was considerable doubt about the authenticity of the radar echoes, President Johnson ordered retaliatory strikes. The *Ticonderoga* and *Constellation* launched a total of 64 Crusaders, Skyraiders and Skyhawks to attack North Vietnamese naval bases. The carrier pilots claimed to have set an oil storage depot on fire and damaged 29 ships for the price of one Skyhawk, whose pilot was taken prisoner.

As a result of the 'Gulf of Tonkin Resolution' Congress gave President Johnson authority to commit US forces in Vietnam, and once again Task Force 77 was formed out of Seventh Fleet units. The two carriers already on station were reinforced by the *Ranger*, and the support carrier *Kearsage* was added to deter any threat of submarine activity by the Chinese.

Despite another incident in the Gulf, TF 77 saw no action until February the following year, when the Viet Cong raided airfields in South Vietnam. On the afternoon of 7 February 1965 the carriers *Coral Sea, Hancock* and *Ranger* launched Operation 'Flaming Dart', an attack by 33 aircraft on Dong Hoi barracks, just north of the 17th Parallel. Next day Dong Hoi was attacked again, but neither raid had any deterrent effect on the Viet Cong, who attacked the American helicopter base at Qui Nhon two days later. This

CHAPTER FOUR
Vietnam

provoked 'Flaming Dart II', a strike of 99 aircraft on Chanh Hoa, a base 35 miles north of the DMZ. Again American losses were light: a Crusader and a Skyraider were shot down by gunfire (one pilot captured, the other rescued) and a Skyhawk destroyed after making a forced landing at Da Nang air base.

The Seventh Fleet now began a blockade of the coast in an attempt to stop the flow of supplies and weapons to the Viet Cong. It was a daunting task to patrol 1100 miles while at the same time supporting the forces on land. On 18 March TF 77 joined in Operation 'Rolling Thunder', a doomed attempt to bomb the Ho Chi Minh government to the conference table. The bombing, carried out in conjunction with the US Air Force, was to last for more than three years, when the President halted it in exchange for an agreement to start peace talks.

The first naval strikes were launched from the *Coral Sea* and the *Hancock* in mid-March 1965. Although the Marines and Seabees had

LEFT: The USS *Coral Sea* (CV-43) in the South China Sea during the SE Asia Treaty Organisation (SEATO) exercises in April 1961. Air Group 15 included F3H, F8U, A4D, AD-6 and A3D aircraft.

built a new base at Chu Lai for ground support, the land forces generally suffered from a lack of airfields, and the Navy was asked by General Westmoreland, US Military Assistance Commander, to make good the deficiency. By June that year no fewer than five attack carriers were stationed in the South China Sea.

The original rules of engagement for 'Rolling Thunder' were very strict. Each strike had to be approved by Washington, no follow-up strike was permitted, nor could targets of opportunity be attacked if the main objective was beyond reach. Air-to-air combat was forbidden unless enemy aircraft had behaved with hostile intent. No prestrike photography was allowed either, leading to losses among the reconnaissance aircraft when they came in after an attack had roused the defences.

The opposition was armed with the Soviet SAM-2 'Guideline' missile as well as light and medium caliber guns. The main air threat was from MiG-17s, which first appeared in combat in April 1965. The first MiG-17s were shot down by Phantom F-4Bs from the *Midway* on 17 June, using the Sparrow air-to-air missile. It was a high-technology war, the first in which naval aircraft had to learn defensive tactics against missiles as well as using them offensively.

The mixing of naval and air force strikes led to the establishment of the 'Yankee' and 'Dixie' carrier operating areas. Two or three

carriers would be stationed in the Yankee zone in the Gulf of Tonkin to mount strikes against North Vietnam. Normally one carrier was allocated to Dixie station for strikes against the Viet Cong south of the DMZ. As its name implies, it was to the south to facilitate operations over South Vietnam. As more carriers became available two were kept in the South China Sea as a reserve, alternating with those on Yankee station but available to reinforce if the Chinese chose to reinforce North Vietnam in strength. The Seventh Fleet's Underway Replenishment Groups were also stationed in the South China Sea.

A carrier coming on-station was usually sent to Dixie station to shake down both ship

TOP LEFT: F-4B Phantoms of VF-114 and F-4Gs of VF-213 on the flight deck of the USS *Kitty Hawk* (CVA-63) in 1966.

BOTTOM LEFT: A Sea Sparrow point defense SAM is fired from the after starboard launcher a board the *John F Kennedy* (CVA-67).

TOP RIGHT: Four F8U Crusaders of VF-211 fly over the USS *Hancock* (CVA-19), tailhooks down and ready to land.

CENTER RIGHT: An A -4 Skyhawk engages the barrier after a bad landing on the USS *Oriskany* (CV-34).

BOTTOM RIGHT: An F-4 Phantom circles over the USS *Midway*.

and air wing, practising light deck routines, launching and recovering in the less hectic atmosphere of South Vietnamese air space. Only when the carrier was fully worked up was she moved to Yankee station, where the real air war began, with AA gunfire and ground-to-air missiles (SAMs) and marauding MiGs and air-to-air combat with guns and missiles.

The intensity of air operations might be expected to reveal shortcomings in airframes and weapon systems, but the US Navy's newest attack aircraft, the Grumman A-6A Intruder all-weather bomber, proved a great success. Unlike the A-1 Skyraider and the A-4 Skyhawk the A-6 could locate targets in any weather and deliver a heavy load of bombs. In one attack against the Uong Bi power station in North Vietnam, two A-6s flying from the *Kitty Hawk* dropped 26 1000 pound bombs, leading Radio Hanoi to claim that B-52 bombers had been used. The first Intruders started operations from the *Independence* in July 1965.

Another new aircraft was the E-2A Hawkeye AEW. With its twin turboprop engines, its 24-foot diameter radome rotating above the fuselage and four vertical stabilizers, the Hawkeye was like no other aircraft before or since. Its crew of two pilots and up to four operators provides radar surveillance as well as command and communications for defending fighters and attacking bombers.

Without doubt the most successful carrier aircraft to come out of the Vietnam War was the McDonnell Douglas F-4 Phantom. It first flew in 1960, and developed into an all-purpose aircraft, capable of flying at Mach 2 (over 1400 mph) but lifting 15,000 pounds of ordnance. In its time the Phantom carried out a wider variety of missions than other aircraft type: tactical strike, close air support, long-range interdiction, AA suppression, reconnaissance and fighter defence. Hailed as the 'MiG killer' it destroyed 146 MiGs, and was so successful that the USAF flew its own variant, the F-4E, in Vietnam.

The nuclear-powered *Enterprise* (CVN-65) arrived on Yankee station at the end of 1965, operating two squadrons of F-4 Phantoms, four A-4C Skyhawk squadrons and a squadron of RA-5C Vigilante ex-bombers converted to the reconnaissance role, with additional helicopters and AEW aircraft embarked. The role of the 'Heavy Seven' Vigilantes was to gather information for the carrier's new Integrated Operational Intelligence Center (IOIC), which could then process and distribute data to other carriers.

Ironically it was a World War II aircraft which was most feared by the Viet Cong and the North Vietnamese. The propeller-driven A-1 Skyraider, capable of no more than 318 mph could loiter at treetop height, firing

LEFT: The Grumman A-6 Intruder bomber could locate targets in any weather.

BOTTOM LEFT: Intruders line the deck of the USS *Constellation* (CVA-64) off the coast of North Vietnam.

RIGHT: Flight deck crewmen rush to recue the pilot of a flak-damaged Skyhawk.

BELOW: An A-4 Skyhawk bombs a Vietcong position in South Vietnam.

ABOVE: The F-4 Phantom, regarded as the finest combat aircraft to come out of the Vietnam War.

LEFT: The E-2C Hawkeye provides airborne early warning and controls the carrier's own aircraft.

TOP RIGHT: The AD-3W Skyraider was equipped with the APS-20 radar for AEW and ASW.

CENTER RIGHT: Bombing up Skyraiders with 2.75 inch rockets.

BOTTOM RIGHT: An A-4 Skyhawk prepares for launch.

guns at anything that moved on the ground. The jets could spend very little time on target, whereas the noise of the Skyraiders was sufficient to keep 'Charlie's' head down.

The greater accuracy of the Intruder strikes, however, was matched by stronger North Vietnamese defences. As early as April 1965 photo reconnaissance sorties detected surface-to-air missile (SAM) sites under construction around Hanoi. Their first Navy victim was a Phantom from the *Midway,* shot down by a Soviet SA-2 'Guideline' missile on 24 July that year.

Tactics to defeat the SA-2 were soon perfected. By flying below 1500-2000 feet altitude and by maneuvering sharply as the missile approached, it was possible to defeat the missile's somewhat primitive guidance system. Inevitably more casualties were then caused by the numerous antiaircraft gun batteries, forcing the USAF and US Navy to resort to electronic means of defeating the SAMs. Two methods were used, jamming (electronic countermeasures or EMC) and 'flak suppression' by attacking the tracking radars of the missile batteries. ECM pods were fitted to Intruders, enabling them to confuse the tracker radars, while radar warning receivers alerted aircraft when missile seekers were locking-on. The AGM-45A Shrike anti-radiation missile was programed to fly down the beam of the tracking 'Fansong' radar, homing on its radiated energy. In a typical SAM engagement a warning light glowed on the instrument panel, and the warbling 'samsong' was heard on the headset. This indicated that the Sa-2's 'Fansong' radar had locked on, giving the pilot

TOP: The F-4 Phantom combined high speed with a heavy payload, making it one of the most versatile carrier aircraft ever built.

ABOVE: An A-6 Intruder parked with wings folded on the flight deck.

tion of the air war. Out of this experience came the Air Force's 'Wild Weasel' operating concept, matched by the Navy's development of the Intruder attack aircraft into the EA-6B Prowler, dedicated to the EW mission. Much of today's aerial tactics, notably flak suppression, stems directly from the Vietnam experience, and EW has developed a huge range of techniques and options.

In March 1966 the first Soviet-built MiG-21 interceptor was in action, a Mach 2 delta-wing aircraft armed with twin 23mm cannon and air-to-air missiles. It was a formidable opponent but never gained superiority over the USAF and Navy aircraft. The first MiG-21 destroyed was credited to an F-8 Crusader from the USS *Oriskany* on 9 October 1966. The pilot, Commander Richard Bellinger, was a veteran of World War II and Korea who had been shot down by a MiG-17 the year before. Analysis of air combat was to show that veteran pilots had an edge over most of their younger colleagues.

The most potent weapon against American air attacks was still ground AA gunfire. Literally thousands of 37mm, 57mm and 85mm AA gun mountings were deployed around cities and industrial centers, and they accounted for about 85 per cent of all US aircraft losses. MiG fighters and SAMs accounted for no more than 15 per cent. The threat had been largely discounted since the early 1950s, and it came as an unpleasant shock to the USAF and Navy to discover that modern aircraft were still vulnerable to light flak.

Techniques of air traffic control improved as the war progressed. To avoid the risk of shooting down civil aircraft, which continued to fly close to the war zone, the US Navy stationed cruisers equipped with enhanced communications and plotting facilities to assist in the task. Their fighter controllers earned high praise for their success in vectoring both land-based and carrier aircraft on to raiding MiGs. To them can be attributed the virtual freedom from enemy air attack enjoyed by the carriers, and the lack of incidents involving civil aircraft.

When the Christmas truce was declared on 24 December the ten carriers deployed off Vietnam had flown nearly 57,000 sorties, on which over 100 aircraft had been lost. Losses in aircrew had been heavy, 86 lost and a further 46 rescued. As in Korea great efforts were made to rescue downed aircrew, with helicopters flying deep penetration missions, backed up by fighter patrols in an effort to pluck survivors from the hands of the enemy.

The 37-day Christmas truce had no effect; the North Vietnamese used the respite to strengthen their defenses and make good much of the damage to roads, bridges and

timely warning to start evasive maneuvers and to launch Shrike missiles if embarked.

The first successful strike against a SAM site was achieved in October 1965, when an A-6A Intruder led a group of A-4 Skyhawks against a target north-east of Hanoi. The Intruder jammed the guidance radars and prevented missiles from being fired, allowing the Skyhawks to bomb with precision. All aircraft returned safely to the *Independence*.

The US Navy's F-4 Phantoms operated the long-range Sparrow air-to-air missile but in practice it proved a disappointment. It suffered no technical failure of any significance, but in close combat it proved a poor dogfighting weapon. When the sky was filled with friendly as well as hostile aircraft it was all too easy to score an 'own goal' by shooting down a friendly aircraft. Many pilots pressed for a return to guns and preferred the short-range Sidewinder missile for aerial combat.

Although shrouded in secrecy at the time, the 'electronic war' was the principal innova-

railways. The result was that when bombing began again in January 1966 the carrier strikes ran into fiercer opposition. By October nearly 400 Navy and Marine Corps aircraft had been lost, and the intensity of operations was causing serious shortages in aircraft, equipment and personnel.

Intensity of operations was also reflected in a serious accident aboard the *Oriskany*. On 26 October 1966 a number of parachute flares being returned to store were ignited accidentally when one of the flares exploded. The fire which resulted spread through the hangar and four decks, killing 44 crewmen and aircrew.

In July the following year the *Forrestal* suffered an even worse fire, when a Zuni rocket under the wing of a Phantom was accidentally fired into the fuel tank of a Skyhawk. The aft—end of the carrier was rapidly engulfed in fire, exploding ordnance and burning aircraft. The main fire was extinguished in an hour but secondary fires burned for another 12 hours. In the holocaust 134 crewmen were killed, while 21 aircraft were destroyed and 43 damaged. The carrier was incapable of operational flying and returned to the US for repairs costing $72 million.

In January 1969 the *Enterprise* while exercising off Hawaii before heading for Vietnam suffered a very similar accident, but revised fire precautions ensured that the fire only lasted three hours. Nevertheless 28 crewmen died and 15 aircraft were destroyed; repairs cost $56 million. The lack of a serious surface or air threat to the carriers had undoubtedly led to a reduction in flight deck safety standards, and the temptation to speed up the rate of sorties meant that a danger-

TOP RIGHT: Arming aircraft in the hangar of the USS *Bon Homme Richard* (CVA-31) off the Vietnam coast in August 1965.

RIGHT: The scene of devastation on the flight deck of the *Forrestal* (CVA-59) in 1967. An accidentally fired Zuni rocket hit a fuel tank and set off an explosion and fires. Repairs cost $72m and 134 crewmen were killed.

ously large amount of ordnance was stored on deck during flying operations. However, it is significant that none of the three carriers came close to being sunk by fires which would probably have destroyed a World War II carrier.

The fire in the *Enterprise* wrecked the after part of the ship's flight deck, but aircraft parked at the forward end were unharmed. As the two forward steam catapults were still functioning she could in theory have continued to launch aircraft, although the destruction of all arrester gear would have prevented her from recovering any, if damage control parties had been unable to rig replacements. It was a graphic demonstration of how much punishment a big carrier can sustain. One authority has described a carrier as a volcano waiting to explode, but a volcano which can be contained by good damage control.

In 1967 attacks on rail and road communications were stepped up. In February A-6A Intruders flew off the *Enterprise* on the first minelaying mission, to deny the Song Ca and South Giang rivers to enemy river transport. In April the first strikes against MiG bases

were authorized, drawing the North Vietnamese Air Force into the conflict on a growing scale. But in spite of huge losses inflicted on the enemy, victory seemed as far off as ever, and the hopes of 'bombing Hanoi to the conference table' looked forlorn. The apostles of strategic air power had learned nothing from World War II. Air power, for all its awesome might, has not rendered other forms of warfare obsolete, and cannot win a war unaided.

Properly used, ground attack and close support continued to be very effective. It was decisive in helping US and ARVN troops to defeat the Viet Cong Tet Offensive, the last occasion on which the VC took the field as a fighting force. When the US Marines established a forward fortified position at Khe Sanh near the Laotian border hostile sections of the US media were quick to predict an 'American Dien Bien Phu', but the defenders fought off a 71-day siege with the support of 1600 sorties by carrier aircraft as well as resupply missions by helicopters and fixed-wing aircraft and bombing raids by B-52 Stratofortress bombers.

The failure of the Tet Offensive had much

BELOW: A flight deck officer directs a Phantom pilot into position before launch from the USS *Saratoga* (CVA-60). December 1972 saw the heaviest raids to date but still the Vietnam War dragged on.

to do with Hanoi's sudden interest in President Johnson's March offer to stop the bombing, but 'Rolling Thunder' continued to the end of October. When the bombing stopped at 8 am on 1 November, nearly a thousand US aircraft had been destroyed, more than 300,000 sorties had been flown, 860,000 tons of bombs had been dropped and the cities and factories of North Vietnam were in ruins. An estimated 52,000 civilians had died, and in theory three-quarters of North Vietnam's military capacity had been destroyed. And yet it had all achieved nothing.

American public opinion had lost faith in the ability of its military forces to win, but the new President Richard Nixon had to grapple with the problem of bringing the conflict to an end without admitting defeat. Task Force 77 aircraft still patroled the skies over South Vietnam, south of the DMZ, but the purpose had gone out of the war. It was still danger-

ous to fly over Vietnam, but the aircrew found the limited objectives particularly frustrating. There was a brief surge of activity in support of a South Vietnamese incursion into Laos in February 1971, but most of the operations were 'truck busting' along the Ho Chi Minh Trail.

Early in 1972 the North Vietnamese started to bring mobile SAMs up to the DMZ, provoking counterstrikes from the two carriers on Yankee station, the *Coral Sea* and *Constellation*. In February the *Hancock* joined them, just in time for the North Vietnamese Army's last roll of the dice. On 30 March three divisions crossed the DMZ, the first of twelve to be committed. If North Vietnam's leaders thought that President Nixon lacked resolution they were mistaken, for the US government unleashed Operation 'Linebacker', an aerial counteroffensive of even greater ferocity than anything previously

ABOVE: *Enterprise* crewmen examine a hole in the flight deck after a fire and explosion during a training exercise in January 1969. Despite severe damage and casualties the nuclear carrier was recommissioned four months later.

seen. With two more carriers rushed to the area, the US Navy struck at targets all over the country, ranging far and wide. On 9 May three A-6A Intruders and six A-7E Corsair IIs from the *Coral Sea* dropped 36 Mk 52 Mod 2 mines in Haiphong harbor. This raid was followed by others against lesser harbors, and immediately all seaborne traffic stopped. During the next eight months USN and USMC aircraft laid 11,000 Mk 36 mines and a further 100 Mk 52s in the approaches to North Vietnamese ports.

In the words of the Chairman of the Joint Chiefs of Staff, Admiral Thomas H Moorer, not one ship left these harbors until the USN undertook clearance operations a year later. Moorer maintained that if his advice had been followed Haiphong would have been mined eight years earlier. Vice-Admiral William P Mack, Commander of the Seventh

Fleet, went further, claiming that all traffic other than the overland route from China was stopped. 'Within ten days', he said, 'there was not a missile or a shell being fired at us from the beach. The North Vietnamese ran out of ammunition just as we always said they would'.

The ceasefire agreement was signed on 23 January 1973, and with it began the final decay of popular will. As the Americans started to pull out, leaving in their place the euphemism 'Vietnamization', both army and civilian morale collapsed disastrously. While the air forces continued to pound the Ho Chi Minh Trail and engaged the North Vietnamese MiGs, the ARVN ground defences crumbled. The inexorable advance of 120,000 troops closed the net on Saigon, and by 7 April 1975 North Vietnamese artillery was shelling the capital.

RIGHT: An F-8A Crusader hooked to the port catapult of the USS *Independence* (CVA-62). This venerable aircraft is still flying from French Navy carriers.

BELOW: An F-8 Crusader ready for launching from the deck of the USS *Oriskany* (CV-34). The steam catapult was retrofitted to many of the older carriers.

As in all military disasters it was now *sauve qui peut,* and it was left to the US Navy carriers to airlift as many refugees as they could. USMC helicopters laid on Operation 'Eagle Pull' to remove embassy staff, and 'Frequent Wind' used 60 CH-53 helicopters to lift the remaining 1500 Americans. Little could be done for the hapless South Vietnamese officials, police, informers and Viet Cong deserters and others who tried to get away.

Although the Vietnam War brought ruin to both halves of the country and cost untold civilian and military casualties, the US Navy and its carriers could be proud of their dedication and heroism. Out of the experience came a new awareness of the limitations of existing weapon systems, but also another lease of life for the big carrier. The enormous impact of electronic warfare has already been touched upon, but there was also a slow realization that deep penetration of hostile air space was becoming too dangerous. The SAM threat had only been contained because of the crudeness of the Soviet systems supplied to North Vietnam. Combined with the demonstration of what massed flak could do to low-flying aircraft, it speeded up the development of new 'smart' weapons capable of being delivered out of range of defensive systems.

Paradoxically the carriers had not been used in the manner for which they had been designed. Instead of 'hit and run' tactics they were forced to remain on-station, maintaining combat air patrols and sorties until aviation fuel and ordnance stores were exhausted. They then withdrew to replenish before returning to the battle zone. While reflecting yet again the inherent flexibility of carriers, it confirmed the US Navy in its preference for nuclear-powered carriers, which could dedicate much more internal space to aviation stores of all kinds.

Critics of the big carrier frequently remind their audience that the Soviet Navy had shown no interest in carriers. That facile argument received a fatal blow when the Soviets showed that they too had decided to build big fixed-wing carriers. But the process had begun much earlier, with the construction of two 'helicopter cruisers' in the 1960s.

The 17,500-ton *Moskva* and *Leningrad* were interesting hybrids, with the armament of a missile cruiser forward (two twin SA-N-3 'Goblet' launchers) and a hangar and flight deck aft, separated by a centerline superstructure and funnel. The air group consisted entirely of 14 Kamov Ka-25 'Hormone-A' ASW helicopters.

In 1975 the West was thrown into consternation by the appearance of a much larger cruiser-carrier. The *Kiev* displaces over 37,000 tons and has a starboard island and angled flight deck to operate a mixed air group of 12 Yak-26 'Forger' VSTOL aircraft, and 22 Ka-25 'Hormone-A' and 'Hormone-B' helicopters. Like the *Moskva* class her forecastle was reserved for a heavy missile armament, but these were SS-N-12 'Sandbox' anti-ship missiles, and the SA-N-3 'Goblet' SAMs were positioned on the island superstructure.

The appearance of the *Kiev* proved that the Soviet planners had finally admitted that organic air defense was necessary if their expanding fleet was to be capable of operating in distant waters. The 'Forger' is, however, not a high-performance aircraft and can only perform a vertical takeoff rather than a rolling takeoff, a severe limitation on endurance. It is in fact a VTOL (vertical takeoff and landing) aircraft rather than a true STOVL type. The 'Hormone' does not compare well with Western ASW helicopters either.

Two more sisters followed, the *Minsk* in 1978 and the *Novorossiisk* in 1982, confirming Western assessments that their main task is to back up long-range anti-submarine groups hunting for Western strategic submarines (SSBNs). Like the *Kiev* they were built in the Black Sea at the Nosenko 444 shipyard in Nikolayev. As early as 1978 reports circulated of a fourth unit, confirmed when the *Baku* was sighted in January 1987.

The *Baku* is basically identical to her sisters, but her superstructure has been remodeled to accommodate a new planar radar similar to the US Navy's Aegis SPY-1A. The number of SS-N-12 'Sandbox' missiles has been increased and the SA-N-3 'Goblets' have given way to vertically launched SA-N-9 SAMs, but the air group remains the same.

In 1979 the US naval intelligence community revealed the existence of a new carrier, possibly nuclear powered and displacing 75,000 tons. Codenamed 'Kreml' (Kremlin)

by Western intelligence, the ship was rumored to be named *Leonid Brezhnev*. However, the death of Brezhnev and later denunciations of his shortcomings makes such a name unlikely; she emerged in late 1989 as the *Tbilisi*.

A second CV, the *Riga* was laid down in 1985, but both ships are believed to be 60,000 tonners and are not nuclear-powered. The *Tbilisi* trials at the end of 1989, but will not be operational for another two years. Her sister will be operational in the mid-1990s. The air group is said to include 12 Yak-41 STOVL aircraft, Ka-27 'Helix' ASW helicopters and a naval version of the Su-27 'Flanker'. To accommodate such a mixed bag the Soviet designers have produced a hybrid C/STOL

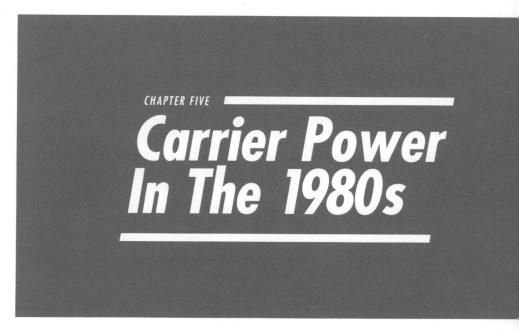

CHAPTER FIVE

Carrier Power In The 1980s

carrier, with a through deck, catapult and arrester wires, and a ski jump offset to port. Western sources now credit the ships with gas turbine propulsion rather than nuclear or steam plant.

To complicate matters the Soviets have now confirmed reports that they are building a third carrier at Nikolayev. The *Ulyanovsk* will displace some 75,000 tons and will probably be nuclear-powered. In one respect she may differ radically from Western supercarriers. Instead of having an attack capability she may be intended as a 'floating airfield' for use by defending land-based fighters to extend their range. Land-based aircraft will, it is claimed, land to refuel and rearm.

For the US Navy the problems are quite different. Although the Vietnam War apparently vindicated the decision to entrust the main offensive capability to naval aviation the cost of maintaining 15 carrier battle groups (CBGs) is high. By the end of 1989 the last of the modernized *Essex* class

LEFT: The Soviet hybrid cruiser-carrier *Kiev* shows her massive armament of eight SS-12 'Sandbox' missiles on the foredeck, and the prominent angled deck with six landing spots. Her three sisters show various improvements as the Soviets gain experience in flying at sea.

were relegated to training or reserve. The *Lexington* cruises in the Gulf of Mexico while the *Bon Homme Richard* and *Oriskany* are in reserve. The carrier battle groups are built around the eight oil-fueled *Forrestal*, *Kitty Hawk* and *John F Kennedy* classes, the two surviving *Midway* class and five nuclear-powered carriers. The *Midway* and *Coral Sea* have been repeatedly modernized but the last overhaul of the *Midway* in Japan was not a success, reducing seaworthiness and her ability to operate aircraft in bad weather.

Clearly both ships will have to be replaced, but the numbers game complicates the issue. Under the 600-ship Navy program initiated by the Reagan Administration, the policy of running 15 CBGs was upheld, but this figure includes the CV or CVN in overhaul. Replacements for the two old carriers are now very urgent.

To keep the *Forrestals* in frontline service they have been given Service Life Extension Programs (SLEPs). The first was the *Saratoga* in 1980-83, followed by the *Forrestal* in 1983-85 and the *Independence* in 1985-88. The fourth ship, the *Ranger*, will receive her SLEP in 1993-95. The *Kitty Hawk* began her SLEP at the beginning of 1988 and will rejoin the fleet in 1991. The *Constellation*'s SLEP will run from 1990 to 1993, the *America*'s

from 1996 to 1999 and the *Kennedy*'s from 1999 to 2002.

Just how expensive a SLEP is can be gauged by the uproar over the SLEP planned for the nuclear-powered *Enterprise*. Her SLEP is planned for 1991-94 at an estimated cost of $2 billion; $465 million has already been spent on long-lead items such as new reactor cores, and a further $600 million on destoring and deactivating the ship. Yet a new CVN would cost $3.3 billion, and the SLEP will give the USS *Enterprise* another 20 years of effective life. After considerable debate Congress finally approved the expenditure in 1989.

Since 1975 the US Navy has commissioned four more nuclear-powered carriers, the *Nimitz, Dwight D Eisenhower, Carl Vinson* and *Theodore Roosevelt*. They are very similar in design and layout to the earlier supercarriers, with more efficient nuclear plants than the *Enterprise*. In fiscal year 1983 two more slightly improved designs were funded, the *Abraham Lincoln* (CVN-72) and *George Washington* (CVN-73), and a further two in 1988 and 1989, the *John C Stennis* (CVN-74) and *United States* (CVN-75). They will be ready in 1998, and will replace the *Midway* and the *Forrestal,* leaving a total of 17 carriers.

Although the big carriers dominate the scene the US Navy's amphibious warfare forces include a considerable air element as well. The five *Tarawa* class amphibious assault ships (LHAs) operate up to 22 Marine Corps AV-8A Harrier STOVL aircraft for close support, supplementing the older *Iwo Jima* class LPHs, which can operate up to four AV-8As. Following them will be the five *Wasp* class multipurpose assault ships

(LHDs), which will operate up to twenty AV-8Bs. Both the LHAs and the LHDs are bigger than most carriers, with full-length flight decks. The AV-8B Harrier II is currently replacing the AV-8A as the standard USMC close-support aircraft. Even the smaller LPHs are flexible; one of them operated minesweeping helicopters in the Persian Gulf in 1987.

USN carriers have been in action twice in recent years, once in 1980 in a disastrous attempt to release hostages held by Iranian fundamentalists in Teheran, the other a punitive strike against Libya. On 4 November 1979, shortly after the fall of the Shah, militant Islamic students stormed the US Embassy in Teheran and took 66 officials and marine guards prisoner. Although 13 were later released the fate of the remaining 53

TOP: The third unit of the *Kiev* class is the *Novorossiisk,* seen here in 1983.

ABOVE: Many Soviet warships operate the Kamov Ka-25 'Hormone' helicopter.

RIGHT: The USS *Nimitz* (CVN-68) was the first of a new class of nuclear powered carriers.

aroused great anger in the United States. Eventually President Carter approved Operation 'Eagle Claw' in April 1980, using special forces to storm the embassy and release the hostages.

The plan was immensely complex, with the special forces (Delta Force) flying in USAF aircraft to a landing site and then storming the embassy. Navy RH-53D Sea Stallion helicopters would then fly into Teheran to airlift the hostages to safety. The eight helicopters took off from the nuclear carrier *Nimitz* cruising in the Gulf of Oman. Bad luck

dogged the operation from the start; one Sea Stallion suffered a serious defect and had to make a forced landing. A second helicopter flew the crew back to the carrier, reducing the force to seven. Desert sandstorms then forced two Sea Stallions to land. Both took off once more but one had to return to the *Nimitz*, reducing the force to six helicopters. When they finally arrived at Desert One, the designated airstrip 300 miles south-east of Teheran, they were over an hour late. Major defects reported by one of the helicopters now eliminated the last hope of getting the hostages out, and 'Eagle Claw' was aborted.

So far the operation had gone undetected but as one of the remaining five Sea Stallions took off it crashed into a KC-130 tanker. Both aircraft burst into flames, killing eight crewmen and injuring five more. Although Delta Force was airlifted out safely the fiasco gave a huge propaganda boost to the Iranians and heightened the American public's sense of outrage. Undoubtedly the incident helped to ensure the defeat of President Carter by Ronald Reagan in the presidential elections later that year.

Another dispute was brewing between the United States and Libya, whose erratic ruler Colonel Qaddafi claimed the Gulf of Sirte as Libyan territory. In August 1981 two carrier battle groups, based on the *Forrestal* and the

Nimitz, were ordered to perform routine exercises in the Gulf of Sirte, challenging Qaddafi's claim to what the US regarded as international waters.

On 19 August two F-14 Tomcat fighters of the CAP were warned by the *Nimitz* that two Sukhoi-22 'Fitter' aircraft were heading for them. The Libyans fired an air-to-air missile out of range, and the Tomcats fired Sidewinders in retaliation. One Su-22 burst into flames, and the other was hit by a 'dud', causing the pilot to eject.

The incident did nothing to dampen Colonel Qaddafi's enthusiasm for terrorist causes, and he continued to be a thorn in the side of the US government. The hijacking of the Italian cruise liner *Achille Lauro* in October 1985 provided further provocation, when an elderly American passenger was brutally murdered and thrown overboard. Although the hijackers were given safe passage out of Egypt, their aircraft was forced down in Sicily by six Tomcats from the USS *Saratoga,* a high-handed action which none the less won universal approval from the American public.

But international terrorism continued and within two months there were bomb attacks at Rome and Vienna airports. Convinced that Libya was behind these attacks President Reagan ordered another demonstration of

LEFT: Sidewinder AIM-9L air-to-air missiles on a Royal Navy FRS.1 Sea Harrier.

BELOW: A Libyan Su-22 'Fitter' seen by US aircraft during a confrontation over the Gulf of Sirte.

BOTTOM: F-14 Tomcat swing-wing fighters.

naval might in the Gulf of Sirte. Operation 'Prairie Fire' involved three carriers of the Sixth Fleet, the *America, Coral Sea* and *Saratoga,* which steamed into the Gulf across Qaddafi's 'Line of Death' between Misratah and Benghazi.

In all, four SAMs were fired at patroling aircraft, all of which missed. Libyan MiGs approaching the carriers were chased off by the CAP, but at about 8 pm a missile-armed patrol boat was spotted approaching. A-6 Intruders fired Harpoon missiles at her, leaving her dead in the water and on fire. A Corsair scored a hit on the Ghurdabiyah SAM position with a HARM anti-radiation missile. At 10 pm the action-packed day ended with a strike by Intruders with Harpoons and laser-guided bombs against a Soviet-built 'Nanuchka' type corvette. Just after midnight the cruiser *Yorktown* fired Harpoons at another missile boat, and later that day aircraft drove off more missile boats. A rational ruler might have seen the folly of such a one-sided engagement but Qaddafi continued to tell the Libyan people that his armed forces were beating the Americans. In April further terrorist acts occurred in Europe, but the response this time was much heavier. USAF aircraft took off from bases in Britain and bombed Tripoli, while Sixth Fleet carrier aircraft attacked Benghazi.

Although international opinion was almost uniformly hostile to the American action, it did seem to deter Qaddafi from further overt encouragement of international terrorist groups. Presumably his military advisers were not prepared to see their entire armory destroyed, and persuaded their eccentric leader to play a quieter role in the future.

TOP: The AIM-7 Sparrow and the AIM-9 Sidewinder are standard US Navy air-to-air missiles.

ABOVE: The variable geometry F-14 Tomcat flies at Mach 2.4 and reaches an altitude of 50,000ft.

LEFT AND TOP RIGHT: HMS *Hermes* during and after the Falklands conflict.

BOTTOM RIGHT: A BAe F RS.1 Sea Harrier landing with wingtip outriggers down.

After the Royal Navy lost the political battle to build two new CVs there was some talk of abandoning fixed-wing aviation, but the rapid progress made in STOVL aircraft in Britain showed that smaller and cheaper carriers might be feasible. The FRS.1 Sea Harrier design was developed from the P.1127 prototype and the aborted P.1154 supersonic STOVL aircraft, and showed the way ahead. But the political climate was so hostile that the RN's new STOVL carrier had to be ordered as a 'through deck cruiser', and the order for the production model FRS.1 Sea Harrier was not placed until construction of the ship was well advanced.

HMS *Invincible* was afloat in 1977 and two sisters were on order before the government of the day consented to equip the class with Sea Harriers. The wisdom of that decision was demonstrated in 1982, when the two-year-old *Invincible* and the old *Hermes* formed the core of the task force sent to the South Atlantic to recapture the Falklands.

The Argentine landing in the Falklands on 1 April 1982 was supported by the carrier *Veinticinco de Mayo* but thereafter she played little part in the war. In contrast the two British carriers, forming the core of Task Group 317.8, were essential to the success of Operation 'Corporate'. They sailed as

LEFT: An FRS.1 Sea Harrier of 800 Naval Air Squadron, armed with Sidewinder AAMs, ready for takeoff from the *Hermes*.

BOTTOM LEFT: Muster of Royal Marine commandos at dawn in the hangar of HMS *Hermes* as she heads for the South Atlantic, April 1982.

BELOW: A battered but victorious *Hermes* on her return to Portsmouth in July 1982.

early as they could, on 5 April, carrying the Fleet Air Arm's entire force of 19 Sea Harriers, as well as 27 Sea King helicopters. Their first landfall was Ascension Island, 3700 miles from the United Kingdom but still 3300 miles from the Falklands.

Had the Argentines handled their carrier with any verve they might have achieved results, for the *Veinticinco de Mayo* had embarked eight of the navy's ten A-4Q Skyhawks, four of five S-2E Trackers, three out of seven Alouette helicopters and five ASW Sea Kings. The carrier was not yet able to fly off the five Super Etendard strike aircraft recently delivered from France, and indeed the Skyhawks could only be launched if sufficient wind over deck could be guaranteed. Parts for the refurbished steam catapult had not arrived from the British supplier . . .

Two events changed the ARA's views. The first was the RAF 'Blackbuck' raid on 1 May by a single Vulcan bomber on the Port Stanley runway, which raised the specter of the British bombing Buenos Aires. The second was the sinking of the cruiser *General Belgrano* a day later, which convinced the ARA that the carrier too was vulnerable to submarine attack. She had in fact tried to fly off a strike against the British task force but the wind speed was too low, and thereafter she was not permitted to operate at sea.

The Sea Harriers found that the new

AIM-9L mark of the Sidewinder missile was deadly in close air-to-air combat, and the 30mm Aden gun was also valuable. In theory the supersonic Mirages and Daggers could outfly the subsonic Sea Harrier but in practice the smaller and more agile aircraft proved superior. In part this was due to no more than geography; the Argentine aircraft had to engage at nearly maximum range, evening out performance differences and allowing training, tactics and weapons to be decisive.

The Sea Harriers had two tasks, to inflict attrition on the Argentine forces until local air superiority was won, and then to give close support to the troops when they went ashore. They achieved both of these admirably, destroying 30 out of the 70 Argentine aircraft lost for a loss of only six of their own. But the lack of airborne early warning was cruelly felt, and it proved impossible to stop all attackers from getting through. The loss of the destroyers *Sheffield* and *Coventry* and the rollon-rolloff ('ro-ro') ship *Atlantic Conveyor* can be directly attributed to the lack of sufficient warning time. Even when victory was near the Argentine Air Force and Navy aircraft remained dangerous, and Navy Skyhawks were able to cripple two landing ships at Bluff Cove when a communications error left the landing force without air cover.

A notable feature of the Falklands

operation was the degree of improvisation. RAF GR.3 Harriers were hurriedly equipped with Sidewinder missiles to eke out the Navy's Sea Harriers, but saw no air-to-air combat. Before the end of the conflict a Sea King helicopter had been adapted to the AEW role by modifying an air-to-surface Searchwater radar, and other helicopters were dropping chaff as a countermeasure to Exocet anti-ship missiles.

The most impressive conversions were the Ships Taken Up From Trade (STUFT). Several were converted to aircraft transports, with improvised flight decks and windbreaks of stacked containers, others were given flight decks to allow troops to be lifted ashore. Ships like the *Atlantic Conveyor* embarked several helicopters and aircraft wrapped in protective material, but had one Sea Harrier 'spotted' on the flight deck to provide the ship with protection.

After the Falklands conflict the Fleet Air Arm strove to implement the lessons. The ex-STUFT container ship *Astronomer* was given a conversion using American equipment. Designated ARAPAHO, it included a light steel mesh flight deck and a sectioned hangar. The converted ship, named RFA *Reliant,* operated off the Lebanon for a short time but she was not a total success, and was returned to mercantile service.

Her successor was another STUFT veteran,

the ro-ro ship *Contender Bezant*. She was given a much more radical conversion, involving extra watertight subdivision, full radar plotting facilities and communications to allow her to operate with naval vessels. RFA *Argus* is in effect a spare deck for Sea Harriers and helicopters, although her peacetime role is to ferry ASW helicopters out to their deep-sea exercise areas.

Unlike the RN the French Navy has clung to its two CVs fiercely, and their replacement has become a matter of urgency. The keel of a 30,000-ton carrier, to be named *Charles de Gaulle*, was laid in 1989, and she will replace the *Clemenceau* in the mid-1990s. The funding for a sister to replace the *Foch* in 2002 or later can be deferred for a little longer but the *Marine Nationale* cannot hope to maintain a viable carrier force in the next century without two carriers. A bitter argument is developing over the choice of fighter aircraft for the *Charles de Gaulle* and the *Foch*. Industry would like to see a French solution, the Rafale Marine, but the French Navy would like to spend scarce foreign currency on buying the McDonnell Douglas F/A-18.

The Spanish Navy has gone down the same route as the British. After operating the old American CVL *Dedalo* for many years with AV-8A Harriers (known in Spanish service as the Matador), the Spanish Defense Ministry bought the plans for a defunct Sea Control Ship from the US Navy. The SCS had been designed to meet requirements for a small carrier to protect convoys and underway replenishment groups, but like other 'austere' carrier designs it could not compete for funds against the big CVs and CVNs. However, for a small navy like the Spanish the SCS was ideal as a support carrier (CVS).

The new CVS, the *Principe de Asturias*, was officially commissioned in 1989. Her AV-8A Matadors will shortly be replaced by the larger AV-8B 'Bravo',and three of her SH-3D Sea Kings will be AEW models, with the same Searchwater radar as the British AEW Sea Kings. Future plans are to build a second CVS in the late 1990s.

TOP LEFT: Flypast of Sea King ASW helicopters over the old *Ark Royal* at the Jubilee Review in 1977.

LEFT: Sea Harriers and Sea Kings on the deck of HMS *Invincible*.

TOP RIGHT: British carriers in the 1960s were armed with Seacat short range missiles.

CENTER RIGHT: The French carrier *Clemenceau* was completed in 1961.

BOTTOM RIGHT: Her sister *Foch* was completed in 1963, and will serve until the year 2004.

ABOVE: The Spanish Navy's first Harrier II was delivered in 1987. They operate from the new carrier *Principe de Asturias*.

TOP RIGHT: INS *Viraat* (ex-HMS *Hermes*) ready to leave for India in May 1987. Her prominent 'ski jump' improves her payload of her Sea Harriers by 50 percent.

BOTTOM RIGHT: The Sukhoi Su-27 'Flanker' is one of the aircraft 'navalized' to fly from the new Soviet carriers of the *Tbilisi* class.

Italy also entered the carrier game, completing the 14,000-ton CVS *Giuseppe Garibaldi* in 1987. Like the British, the Italian Navy faced political constraints, with the Air Force putting up fierce opposition to naval control over aviation. Although the ship was completed with a full-width ski-jump the Italian Navy was forced to pretend that the device was merely there to improve seakeeping. For the first three years of her life she has been restricted to helicopter operations, although the British Sea Harrier has carried out landing trials. In 1989 after long and bitter wrangling the Naval Law was amended by the Italian Parliament, allowing the Navy to procure and crew its own aircraft; hitherto the Air Force had a monopoly of these two crucial capabilities, but the way is now clear to buy STOVL aircraft. The likely choice is an upgraded version of the McDonnell Douglas AV-8B. A second carrier, to be named *Giuseppe Mazzini*, is planned for the end of the century.

The most remarkable expansion of naval aviation has been seen in the Indian Navy. For years the old British-built CVL *Vikrant* operated as a solitary unit but in 1983 the *Hermes* was bought from the RN and renamed *Viraat*. Both hulls are quite old and it was no surprise when the Indian Navy announced that it would build a replacement for the *Vikrant,* although they have now decided to build three 30-35,000-ton carriers. The design has been awarded to the French *Direction Constructions Navals* (DCN), the official French naval design bureau, and the lead-ship will be laid down at Cochin Shipyard before the end of 1991. The design will be similar to the new Soviet CVs, a combined fixed-wing/STOVL carrier with a ski-jump and a through flight deck to enable her to operate conventional aircraft as well as the FRS.1 Sea Harrier. Unfortunately industrial trouble at Cochin has raised doubts about the yard's ability to deliver the ship in time for the 50th anniversary of India's independence in 1997.

In the meantime the venerable *Vikrant* has been given a ski-jump to improve the performance of her Sea Harriers. Another major improvement is the imminent purchase of Searchwater radars for AEW Sea King helicopters. The likeliest candidate for the new carrier's fixed-wing element is the same Su-27 'Flanker' which will fly from the Soviets' 'Tblisi' type.

The next navy to move into the carrier business may be the Japanese Maritime Self Defense Force (JMSDF). A political row was sparked off when the subject arose at the end of the 1980s, with the Opposition claiming that the Constitution forbids the construction of 'offensive' warships, the construction of a CVS would make a lot of sense. The JMSDF is dedicated to ASW, and the increased performance of submarines makes it essential to use helicopters at longer ranges. At present the JMSDF operates Sea King ASW helicopters off large destroyers (DDHs) but there is a practical limit to the efficiency of such a small air group.

A CVS, possibly based on the Sea Control Ship design supplied to Spain, would permit ASW hunting groups to keep helicopters flying longer at a smaller cost than present. The Director General of the Bureau of Defense Policy has also clarified the constitutional position, pointing out that a light ASW carrier is not illegal. Two new LPDs are reported to be capable of operating STOVL aircraft, perhaps an interim solution.

Rather more offensive is the reported interest of the People's Liberation Army (PLA) Navy in acquiring the two laid-up *Essex* class carriers from the US Navy. No firm evidence is offered by China watchers but the Chinese

press has in recent years harped on the lack of aircraft carriers, and it is claimed that a training course for carrier COs has been running at a naval academy in Guangzhou province. The tragic events in Tiananmen Square have destroyed the fragile relationship between Beijing and the West, but there is no doubt that the West would still prefer the PLA Navy to buy Western rather than Soviet naval aviation expertise. The purchase of the *Bon Homme Richard* and *Oriskany* would make sense for the PLA Navy, while releasing very little up-to-date technology.

As the 1980s drew to a close it was clear that carrier warfare, far from being obsolete, was thriving. The US Navy was vindicated in its continuing faith in the big carrier, while the Fleet Air Arm was rejuvenated by the advent of STOVL technology. It is too early to analyze the full impact of the Soviet carrier plans – the carrier program seems to have escaped defense cuts made as part of *perestroika* – but if Soviet carrier battle groups take to the oceans things will never be the same.

The future of the large carrier is by no means secure. Its colossal cost makes it unpopular, and critics attack its supposed vulnerability. However, the US Navy's carrier battle groups are indisputably the only means, other than submarines, of carrying the offensive to the Warsaw Pact should war ever break out between the Western Alliance and the Soviet Bloc.

That simple fact will keep the US Navy's carriers intact for the next decade. All warships are vulnerable, but a large carrier, properly handled and given the right assets to defend it, should survive better than lesser warships. The threat from anti-ship missiles does not invalidate the concept of an attack carrier but it does raise its cost, in much the same way that the torpedo threat made battleships more costly at the turn of the century.

Paradoxically, considerations such as these make the smaller carrier less attractive as an attack weapon, although specialized ASW ships have a considerable role to play. In any cost-effectiveness exercise the big carrier always wins — it carries more aircraft, more fuel and more ordnance than a medium-sized carrier.

Although the British are justifiably proud of their STOVL innovations there is no real comparison between the performance and capability of a conventional fixed-wing aircraft and those of STOVL aircraft. Although the Royal Navy has a requirement for a supersonic STOVL strike aircraft for the late 1990s, there is still much to be done to improve endurance and payload. It has been said that the Sea Harrier is roughly at the same stage of development as the Sopwith Camel was in 1917 — an interesting comparison, laden with possibilities.

There can be no doubt that a single 60,000-ton carrier with an air group of 80 to 90 high-performance aircraft would have devastated the Argentine Air Force in the Falklands in 1982. Nor should the truth be ignored, that if the Falklands had been only 150 miles closer to Argentina the Fleet Air Arm Sea Harriers would have been defeated.

On balance, therefore, there is no real case for the US Navy (or, for that matter, the Soviets) to abandon the big carrier in favor of some as yet undiscovered rival capital ship. Indeed it can be argued that the two navies should shun any attempt to force them to build smaller, more vulnerable and less effective carriers. To abandon the CV and the CVN is to forego a significant range of capabilities in both peacetime and wartime.

The facts of geography ensure that the crisis points are far away from the home base, making it difficult for a nation lacking aircraft carriers to bring pressure to bear.

The impotence of the Soviet Navy in the Gulf, for example, has irked them for years. Equally the huge logistic effort required to ship Cuban soldiers to Angola could have been frustrated had the American government shown the will to deploy a carrier battle group in the mid-Atlantic.

Although the technology of attack gets most publicity, defense has also made giant strides in recent years. The Aegis fleet defense system, despite criticism after an Aegis-equipped cruiser shot down an Iranian airliner in the Persian Gulf, offers a credible defense against saturation attacks with missiles. It controls all the layers of defense, from the outer layer of the CAP down to the point where area and point defense missiles eliminate all but a few 'leakers'.

The arguments for switching to STOVL are

CHAPTER SIX

The Future

not yet decisive, but in the late 1970s the US Navy looked seriously at a proposal for a STO (Short Take Off) carrier. Using modern techniques such as variable geometry (swing wing) it could be feasible to make a rolling takeoff without the need for a catapult. With a wind over deck speed of, say, 60 knots (30 knots ship speed + 30 knots wind) the length required for takeoff would be cut by over 80 per cent, and a shallow ski-jump would improve those figures.

Even if the STO carrier becomes a reality it would still be a carrier suited to low-threat areas, much like the Sea Control Ship proposed by Admiral Zumwalt in the 1970s. The same can be said of the European support carriers, which are designed to support anti-submarine operations and provide local strike and air superiority. As the British showed in the Falklands, such ships can also serve in out-of-theater operations but they could not take on and defeat a land-based air force in the way that American carrier

LEFT: The veteran carrier *Midway* (CV-41) steaming in the Western Pacific. She has served for 45 years but she is unlikely to be replaced.

ABOVE: A Fleet Air Arm Phantom taking off from the old carrrier HMS *Ark Royal*.

LEFT: Crewmen watch a radar scope in the Combat Information Center of the USS *Ranger* (CV-61).

TOP RIGHT: A Sea Harrier takes off from HMS *Invincible* during the Falklands campaign.

BOTTOM RIGHT: A variety of aircraft ranged on the foredeck of the USS *Carl Vinson* (CVN-70), third of the *Nimitz* class.

aircraft did in Korea and Vietnam.

If the American carrier force is eventually to fall below the level of 14 battle groups merely for lack of funding, and the Western Alliance can be forced to admit that it needs such a force-level, a case could be made for a NATO-funded carrier force. The value of the US Navy's carrier battle groups, particularly in containing the Soviet Northern Fleet in its Arctic bases, rests as much as anything on the number of carriers which could be deployed simultaneously. Put another way, if none of the lesser navies could afford to build and operate a single big carrier, a pooled carrier force might be an alternative.

More serious in the short term is the effect of budget cuts on aircraft procurement. The recently retired Chief of Air Warfare, Vice-Admiral Robert F Dunn, pointed out in 1989 that plans to cut the advanced tilt-rotor V-22 Osprey aircraft would seriously hamper the US Marine Corps. He also predicted that the carrier force would be short of 56 F-14 Tomcats by the end of the century, risking a shortfall while the Advanced Tactical Fighter (ATF) becomes operational.

Other cancelations include the A-6F Intruder, which left the Grumman Corporation with only a small amount of work. The withdrawal of Grumman from naval work would leave McDonnell Douglas the only manufacturer of carrier aircraft in the USA, a far cry from the buoyant industry of the 1970s.

These arguments are really confined to the superpowers. Smaller navies with narrower objectives still feel the need for the benefits of carrier air power, and they will continue to seek solutions. The small number of carriers still serving in minor navies are all old, and replacement is becoming urgent. One solution is a capable mercantile conversion such as the British RFA *Argus*. Large mercantile hulls are comparatively cheap, and it would also be possible to build to a mercantile design if the cost of conversion seemed too expensive. What cannot be done is to achieve a major capability without spending money. The air group alone costs billions of dollars: the SLEP overhauls for CVs and CVNs equal the annual budget of many navies.

Whatever the critics may say, the might of a carrier battle group remains one of the most awe-inspiring sights in the world today. Her attendant destroyers and cruisers provide mutual defense as well as formidable offensive capability. The Soviets will take a long time to reach the operational efficiency of the US Navy, but when they do, the world may see the first carrier vs. carrier battles since World War II.

PREVIOUS PAGE: The USS *America* (CV-66) berthing at Pearl Harbor. It is perhaps fitting that the USS *Arizona* memorial in the background marks the destruction of the battle fleet which gave carrier tactics their chance.

BELOW: The new Soviet carrier *Tbilisi* leaves the Nikolaiev shipyard bound for Sevastopol. Her sister *Riga* will be followed by two larger CVNs.